Ka-52/K ALLIGATOR/KATRAN

Scout (Reconnaissance)/Attack Helicopter

HUGH HARKINS

Copyright © 2018 Hugh Harkins

All rights reserved.

ISBN: 1-903630-746
ISBN-13: 978-1-903630-747

Ka-52/K
Alligator/Katran

Scout (Reconnaissance)/Attack Helicopter

© Hugh Harkins 2018

Centurion Publishing

United Kingdom

ISBN 10: 1-903630-746
ISBN 13: 978-1-903630-747

This volume first published in 2018

The Author is identified as the copyright holder of this work under sections 77 and 78 of the Copyright Designs and Patents Act 1988

Cover design © Createspace Independent Publishing Platform & Centurion Publishing

Page layout, concept and design © Centurion Publishing

All rights reserved. No part of this publication may be reproduced, stored in a retrieval system, transmitted in any form, or by any means, electronic, mechanical or photocopied, recorded or otherwise, without the written permission of the publisher

The publisher and author would like to thank all organisations and services for their assistance and contributions in the preparation of this volume: Central Aerodynamic Institute, TsAGI; JSC Concern Kalashnikov ; JSC Alloy; JSC Aviaavtomatika; JSC GosMKB Vympel; JSC Klimov; JSC Scientific and Production Association NPO Splav; KBP Tula; Kret; NPP Zvezda; Phazotron NIIR; OJSC Plant VA Degtyareva; RCC Roscosmos; RPKB Ramenskoye; Rosoboronexport; Rostec Corporation; Russian Helicopters; Tulamashzavod Production Association, Ministry of Defence of the Russian Federation and Defence Intelligence Agency

CONTENTS

	INTRODUCTION	i
1	KA-52 DESIGN LINEAGE	1
2	KA-52/K DESIGN & SYSTEMS	11
3	KA-52/K WEAPONS COMPLEX	57
4	KA-52/K SERVICE ENTRY & OPERATIONAL DEPLOYMENT	73
5	GLOSSARY	83

INTRODUCTION

The intent of this volume is to detail the Kamov (Russian Helicopters) Ka-52 Alligator and its naval analogue, the Ka-52K Katran, многоцелевой ударо-разведывательный вертолет (Multi-purpose Strike and Reconnaissance Helicopter) from a systems, sensors, defensive aids and armament viewpoint. It is not intended as a historical monograph of the Ka-50 program that led to the Ka-52, although a short historical background will be furnished in the opening chapter. Subsequent chapters will focus on the technical systems, sensors, defensive aids and armament of the land based and maritime variants. A brief resume of the service entry and operational history of the land based and maritime variants will be furnished, including brief details of operations in the Syrian Arab Republic in 2016-2017.

1

KA-52 DESIGN LINEAGE

In 2016, the Ka-52 Alligator and Ka-52K Katran многоцелевой ударо-разведывательный вертолет (Multi-purpose Strike and Reconnaissance Helicopter) were committed to combat operations against ISIL (Islamic State of Iraq and the Levant), Al Nusra Front and other aligned opposition groups that had, over the previous few years, overrun large swathes of the territory of the Syrian Arab Republic. The Ka-52 had entered service with the Russian Air Force in 2011, and, in late 2016 through early 2017, the Ka-52K had achieved an operational trials capability of two aircraft with Russian Naval Aviation.

The Ka-52, developed from the Ka-50, was the latest in a line of co-axial rotor helicopters designed and developed by Kamov (Kamov since 2008, formerly, 1991-2008, Kamov Helicopter Scientific Complex and Ukhtomsky Helicopter Plant from 1974-1991). The first purpose designed naval aircraft developed by the Soviet Union, the Ka-25 (allocated the NATO (North Atlantic Treaty Organisation) reporting name 'Hormone') ASW (Anti-Submarine Warfare) and general purpose helicopter, was also the first co-axial rotor helicopter designed with a clear armed warfare function. The Ka-25, the prototype of which had conducted its maiden flight on 26 April 1961, was derived from earlier Kamov designs, in particular the Ka-15 (this design conducted its maiden flight in 1953) and the Ka-18 (this design conducted its maiden flight in 1957) light utility helicopters, which were developed from the Ka-10 that had conducted its maiden flight in 1949. This latter design had proved the co-axial rotor concept that would be refined and incorporated on future Kamov designs, including the aforementioned Ka-15/Ka-18 & Ka-25, as well as a host of other designs of the extended Ka-27/28/29/31/32 families, the Ka-50 and Ka-52. The Kamov co-axial rotor designs were produced serially at the Ulan Ude Aviation Plant in the South eastern Soviet Union (now within the Russian Federation).

Development of the design that would emerge as the Kamov Ka-50 had commenced in 1976, the same year of the maiden flight of the prototype of Kamov's first helicopter designed to engage ground targets, the Ka-29 naval assault transport. The prototype of the Ka-50 (allocated the NATO reporting name 'Hokum'), which was designated V-80 (also known within Kamov and the USSR (Union of Soviet Socialist Republics) Defence Ministry as the Product 800), conducted its maiden flight on 17 June 1982 - pilot Nikolay Bezdetnov. The flight was conducted under a cloak of great secrecy - the white painted prototype was apparently disguised to look like a small passenger helicopter, complete with outlines of windows and doors painted on the sides. The initial flight test phase was conducted in an equal measure of secrecy, the helicopter being flown either within cloud cover or at night and secured in a hanger when not in flight test.

The two-seat Ka-52 (top) was directly derived from the single-seat Ka-50 (above) that entered service with the Russian Federation Army in 1995. MODRF

Top: The first of a long line of Kamov co-axial rotorcraft to be designed in Soviet Russia emerged as the Ka-10, referred to as the 'Flying Motorcycle', which conducted its maiden flight in 1949. Above: The Ka-10 led to the Ka-15 co-axial light utility helicopter, the prototype of which flew in 1953, a number serving in a naval capacity in the early 1960's, particularly aboard Soviet auxiliary vessels. Russian Helicopters

Top: A Mil Mi-24 prototype development helicopter. Above: A Mi-24A production helicopter. The Mi-24 is often attributed the label of the first Soviet purpose designed attack helicopter. However, in actuality the design, which enthralled western analysts of the 1970's and 1980's, was that of a heavily armed assault/transport helicopter.
Russian Helicopters

Kamov (Russian Helicopters) Ka-29 assault transport (the helicopter shown above served with Naval Aviation of the Russian Federation Baltic Fleet) developed for Soviet, and later serving with Russian Federation naval aviation, was Kamov's first helicopter designed to lay down heavy suppressive fire and engage armoured vehicles. MODRF

The Design studies that led to the Ka-50 were initiated to address shortcomings of the Mi-24 (allocated the NATO reporting name 'Hind') as an attack helicopter. It had been considered within the higher command of the USSR armed forces that the Mi-24 was compromised in the attack helicopter role by its design, which was fundamentally oriented towards that of a heavily armed assault/transport helicopter (Russian Helicopters). It was considered that the assault helicopter design heritage of the Mi-24 would reduce its effectiveness as a dedicated battlefield attack helicopter in comparison to foreign developments typified by the AH-64 Apache (now administered by Boeing).

To address the design of a new generation attack helicopter the Kamov and Mil design bureaus were involved in a number of studies. Mil's design proposal would lead to the Mi-28 (allocated the NATO reporting name 'Havoc') single main rotor stabilising tail rotor battlefield attack helicopter. By contrast, Kamov, under Sergey Mikheev, decided on a new approach that would build on its experience of co-axial rotor helicopter design, which, although being technologically more complex than a traditional single main rotor/stabilising tail rotor design, was considered to carry with it significant advantages (Russian Helicopters).

Incorporation of the co-axial rotor concept allowed the overall length of the new Kamov (Ukhtomsky) attack helicopter to be reduced as it removed the necessity for a stabilising tail rotor and also reduced the required power output as a tail rotor in itself would absorb a not insignificant amount of the overall engine power output. Russian Helicopters writings put forward an increased efficiency value of 22% for a co-axial rotor design over a traditional single main rotor/stabilising tail rotor design, assuming the same main rotor diameters for both designs. Another benefit of the co-axial rotor design identified for the attack helicopter role was negation of a requirement for a lengthy drive shaft through the tail boom, reducing the requirement for armouring to protect such a shaft inherently required in a single main rotor, stabilising tail rotor design. This effectively enhanced combat survivability. Testing had shown co-axial rotor designs to have increased altitude operating characteristics over that of single main rotor/stabilising tail rotor designs, assuming engines of the same specific power and more or less the same operational weights for each design. Overall operating altitude of the co-axial rotor design would be expected to be around 1000 m higher and rate of climb around 5 m/s greater than that of a single main rotor/stabilising tail rotor design off corresponding power and weight. The co-axial design also increased the helicopters maneuverability. The Ka-50 was capable of a number of manoeuvres that no other operational or experimental attack helicopter could emulate. Among these was the 'Funnel' manoeuvre in which the helicopter would fly laterally (sideways) at high speed whilst circling a certain point such as a ground target, all the while being able to keep a continuous fire concentrated on said target.

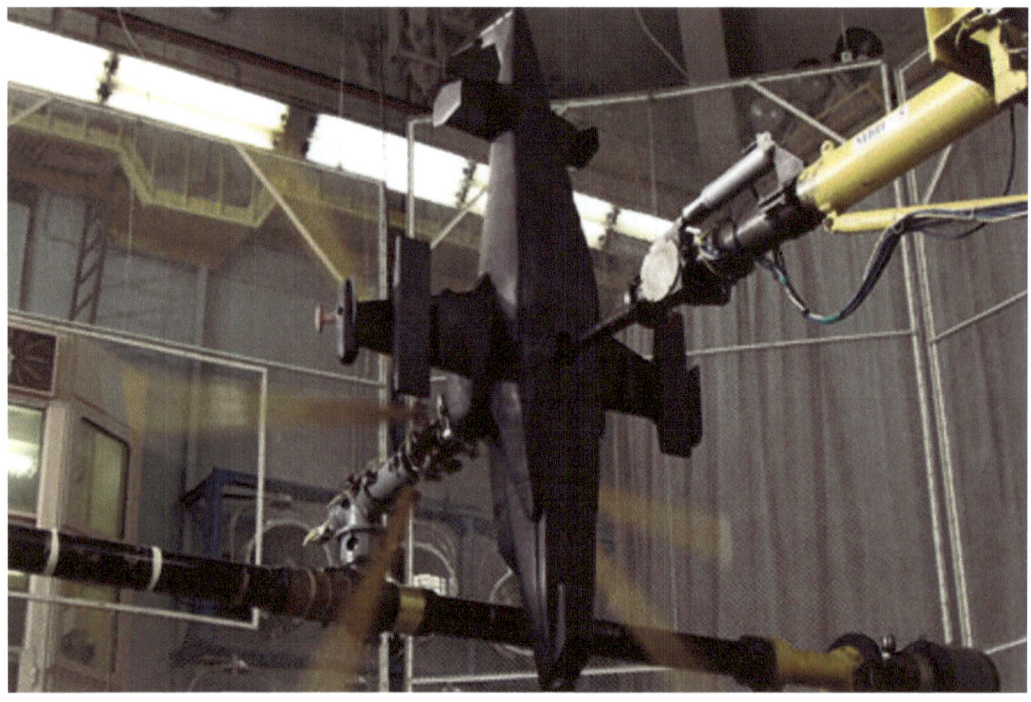

A Ka-50 model in a wind-tunnel complex at TsAGI. TsAGI

A circa mid-1980's US intelligence services depiction of the Ka-50 (NATO reporting name 'Hokum' A) co-axial rotor attack helicopter with a Mi-28 single main rotor/stabilising tail rotor attack helicopter in the lower right of picture. DIA

Russian helicopters documentation indicates that production examples of the Ka-50 were built from 1990 and the design entered Russian Federation army service in 1995. Only a small batch of production standard Ka-50 helicopters (allocated the name Black Shark in 1993) were built for the Soviet Union and its major successor state, the Russian Federation (the Soviet Union was dissolved into a Commonwealth of Independent States on 25 December 1991). Potential further production plans were officially halted in 2009 as design studies had turned toward a more advanced and ultimately more capable all-weather scout/attack helicopter that would itself be derived from the basic Ka-50 – among the planned Ka-50 derivatives was the Ka-50N (a night capable attack helicopter) and the Ka-50-2 Erdogan. Development of the new design, which would emerge as the Ka-52, would draw on operational experience gained by the small force of operational Ka-50's. Two Ka-50's, termed Fire Support Helicopters by the Ministry of Defence of the Russian Federation, had been incorporated into a Russian Federation experimental operational group for combat operations in the Chechnya Republic in December 2000/January 2001, experience of these operations feeding into the Ka-52 program.

Kamov Ka-50 Black Shark Fire Support Helicopter – data furnished by MODRF

Engines: 2 x Klimov TV3-117VMA turboshafts
Thrust of engines: 2 x 2200 hp.
Overall dimensions: 16 x 4.93 m
Rotor diameter: 14.5 m
Maximum take-off weight: 10800 kg
Normal take-off weight: 9800 kg
Basic empty weight: 7692 kg
Maximum mass consumed payload: 1811 kg
Normal mass consumed payload: 610 kg
Maximum flight speed: 300 km/h
Cruising speed: 270 km/h
Ceiling, static: 4000 m
Ceiling, dynamic: 5500 m
Range at normal take-off weight: 460 km
Ferry range: 1160 km
Crew: 1
Weapons: single 2A42 30 mm cannon, guided anti-tank missiles with an automatic laser beam guidance system (can be used against air targets) and unguided rockets

Poor quality photo of a development test example of the Ka-50. Russian Helicopters

Previous page top: A Ka-50 Fire Support (Scout/attack) helicopter on display at the opening day of the Moscow International Air Show at Zhukovsky (formerly known in the west as Ramenskoye) in the 1990's. Previous page top and this page: Ka-50 Black Shark helicopters in service with the Russian Federation. USAF/MODRF

2

KA-52/K DESIGN & SYSTEMS

The Kamov (Russian Helicopters) Ka-52 Alligator is described as a day/night/all-weather SCOUT (reconnaissance)/attack helicopter (also referred to as a Multi-Purpose Strike and Reconnaissance helicopter capable of engaging a wide range of armoured and soft skinned targets. The Ka-52K Katran (катран), which is a variant of the Alligator optimised for the maritime environment, was originally intended for operations from the Mistral Class helicopter carriers ordered to be built for the Russian Federation Navy in France before this program was terminated due to the imposition of European Union sanctions on the Russia Federation following Crimea's reunification with the Russia Federation in 2014. The main role of the Ka-52K is to provide fire support/close air support for naval infantry during amphibious landing operations (MORDF). It is, however, clear that such a variant could be utilised in other roles.

Development of the Ka-52, itself a deep modification of the previous generation Ka-50, had commenced in 1995 under chief designer Sergei Mikheyev. A representation of the new design was presented at the MAKS-1995 Air Salon following acceptance of the concept design, which had been approved on 15 March that year. The prototype of the Ka-52 conducted its maiden flight, in hover, at the flight test facility in Zhulebino, Moscow, on 25 June 1997. Further refinements to the design continued through the late 1990's and early 2000's, resulting in a refined design being presented at MAKS-2003. A further redesign led to the standard variant proposed for production, which had its public debut at the MAKS show in 2007. The Ka-52 was selected for service with the Russian armed forces in 2006, entered serial production on 29 October 2008 and entered service in 2011.

Retaining the Ka-50 power plant, support systems, undercarriage, mid and rear fuselage sections, wings (stub wings) and fins, the Ka-52 introduced a new front fuselage housing the two-crew cockpit and a number of other changes, including 'different-side blade rotation', which enables the helicopter to conduct a manoeuvre referred to as the 'whirlpool'. This 'involves lateral flight moving by vast circle trajectory above the target and down-slope pointing at it' (Rostec). Such manoeuvres have been developed for use in evading active air defences such as a missile homing on the helicopter. This is only one of many high agility manoeuvres able to be performed, it being recognised that the helicopter is endowed with extremely high levels of manoeuvrability, aided, in no small part, by the co-axial rotor configuration, allowing the helicopter to conduct tight manoeuvres, even in environments of spatial limitation.

Previous page top: Ka-52 demonstrator at the Paris Air Salon, Le Bourget airport. Previous page bottom: Graphic depiction of the production standard Ka-52 in flight. This page: The Ka-52/K Alligator/Katran, like their predecessor, the Ka-50 Black Shark, adopted the characteristic co-axial rotor configuration that had been tried, tested and refined on four generations of Kamov helicopters. The co-axial configuration, as well as negating the need for a stabilising tail rotor system, bestows upon the helicopter unrivalled operational maneuverability and a number of other performance plusses such as increased climb rate. Russian Helicopters/MODRF

Top: The co-axial rotor configuration negates the requirement for a complex stabilising tail rotor of the type found on attack helicopters of Russian Helicopters Mi-28N, Boeing AH-64 Apache or Eurocopter (Airbus) Tiger designs. Above: The side-by-side seating configuration is much vaunted by crews over the less operationally flexible tandem layout of the Mi-28N, AH-64 or Tiger. Russian Helicopters/MODRF

The Ka-52 Alligator airframe, engines and onboard systems were extensively tested over a diversity of terrain types and in overwater environments. The land based Ka-52 does not have the additional anti-corrosion protection that would be incorporated in the Ka-52K, which is designed for ship-board deployment. Russian Helicopters

TV3-117VMA & VK-2500 engines – The Ka-52 can be powered by either the JSC TBG Klimov TV3-117VMA (High Altitude Modernised Model 'A') turboshaft engine or the VK-2500 turboshaft engine. Documentation furnished by the MODRF states emphatically that the Ka-52 fleet in service with the Russian Federation Aerospace Forces are powered by two TV3-117VMA engines. Further MODRF documentation indicates that the Ka-52K variant developed for Russian Federation Naval Aviation is powered by two VK-2500 engines, this engine may power late production examples – both engine designs are available for export customers.

The TV3-117VMA turboshaft engine, with a baseline power rating of 2200 hp., was originally developed for the Ka-50 attack helicopter, but also powered other platforms, including the Kamov Ka-27, Ka-29, Ka-31 and the civil Ka-32 helicopters (TV3-117VMA Series 02) as well as non Kamov designs such as Mil Mi-24 models and the Mi-28N attack helicopter - serial production commenced in 1986.

The VK-2500 turboshaft engine, which had been developed by 2001, was intended to power the resurgent Russian attack helicopter programs in the early twenty first century – Ka-52, Mi-28N (such aircraft in Russian Federation service are powered by the TV3-117VMA) and Mi-35M (such aircraft intended for domestic service are powered by the TV3-117VMA), as well as the upgraded Mi-17 assault helicopters and later Ka-27 and Ka-32 updates. The VK-2500, which features a service life of 9,000 hours, develops up to 2400 hp. at take-off (the engine has apparently been rated up to 2700 hp., but 2400 hp. is the baseline rating). Helicopters powered by the VK-2500 have demonstrated operational ceiling increases up to 30%, rate of climb increase of up to 50% and payload increases of 1000-2000 kg (depending on helicopter design), compared with values calculated for other engine types. The engine performance allows increased speeds and manoeuvrability to be achieved by the respective helicopter designs so powered and the design is particularly well suited for operations in high (mountainous) geographic regions and hot climates. The engine provides ample power for routine operations at altitudes in excess of 5000 m, static ceiling being 4000 m. The power ratings are more than adequate to allow the helicopter to take-off, operate and land in hot climates and in high altitude theatres such as mountain ranges as well as routinely operate in cold climates under adverse conditions, including snow and ice.

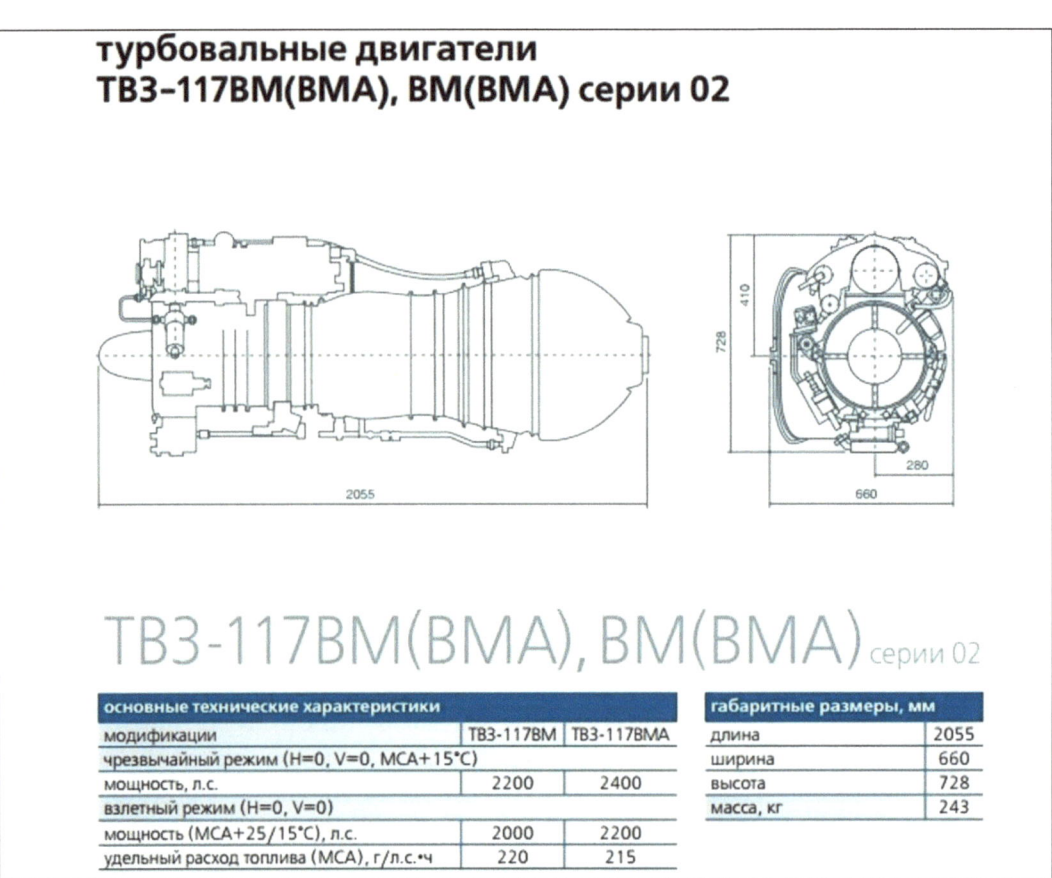

Klimov Russian language diagram, with English translation italicized in parenthesis, detailing the basic characteristics of the TV3-117VM/VMA engines. TV3-117BM/BMV турбовалвные двигатели (*turbo engines*); серии 02 (*series 02*); основные технические характеристики (main technical characteristics); модификации (modifications): тв3-117вм, тв3-117вмА; чрезвычайный режим (*emergency mode*) (H=0, MCA+15° C); мощность, л.с. (*power, h.p.*): 2200 (ВМ) 2400 (ВМА); взлетный режим (*take-off mode*): H=0, V=0; мощность (*power*) (МСА+25/15° C), л.с (hp.): 2000 (ВМ), 2200 (ВМА) удельный расход топлива (*specific fuel consumption*) (МСА г/л.с. ч: 220 (ВМ), 215 (ВМА); габритные размеры, мм (*overall dimensions, mm*); длина (*length*): 2055; ширина (*width*): 660; высота (*height*): 728; масса, кг (*weight, kg*): 243

Top: The Ka-52 stands out from its competitors by, as was the case with the Ka-50, featuring a retractable tricycle undercarriage system. The twin nose wheel retracts aft into the forward fuselage underside while the main wheels retract to tuck into the centre fuselage lateral sections as shown here. Above: A Ka-52 Alligator taxis at the Paris Air Salon at Le Bourget airport in June 2015. The aircraft is adorned with a distinctive black/sand colour scheme. Russian Helicopters

Russian Language graphic, with English translation in parenthesis, depicting the Klimov тв3-117вм (вма) series 02 turboshaft engine

турбовалвные двигатели (turbo engines)
тв3-117вм (вма), вм (вма) серии 02 (series 02)

TV3-117VMA specification – data for Series 02 engine furnished by JSC Klimov

Horsepower
Emergency performance (H=0, V[e]=0)
Power (ISA+150C): 2400 hp.
Takeoff performance (H=0, V[e]=0)
Power (ISA+30/25/150C): 2000 hp., 2200 hp.
Specific fuel consumption, (ISA), g/hp./hour, not higher than: 215
Cruising performance (H=0, V[e]=0)
Power (ISA+25/25/150C): 1500 hp.
Length: 2055 mm
Width: 660 mm
Height: 728 mm
Weight: 295 kg (this conflicts with data on page 16 that states 243 kg)

H=Height
V[e]=Velocity
C=Centigrade

Ka-52/K

Russian Language graphic, with English translation in parenthesis, depicting the Klimov BK-2500 turboshaft engine

турбовалвные двигатели (turbo engines)
вк-2500 (VK-2500)

VK-2500 engine specification – data furnished by JSC Klimov

Horsepower
Emergency performance (H=0, V[e]=0)
Power (ISA+150C): 2700 hp.
Takeoff performance (H=0, V[e]=0)
Power (ISA+30/25/150C): 2000 hp., 2200 hp., 2400 hp.
Specific fuel consumption, (ISA), g/hp./hour, not higher than: 220 (I), 214 (II), 210 (III)
Cruising performance (H=0, V[e]=0)
Power (ISA+25/25/150C): 1500 hp. (I), 1500 (II), 1750 hp. (III)
Length: 2055 mm
Width: 660 mm
Height: 728 mm
Weight: 300 kg

Top: The Ka-52 crew are seated on NPP Zvezda K-37-800M shock-absorbing ejection seats, which form the major component of the CAS-37-800M catapult-cushioning system. Above: Another component of the overall catapult-cushioning system is the ZS-7VS protective helmet adorned by the Ka-52 crew. NPP Zvezda

In regards to armouring of the helicopter, Rosoboronexport described this as a 'heavily armoured cockpit, vital systems and components', it being clear that an emphasis was placed on cockpit armouring for crew protection (Rosoboronexport).

The K-52 can be equipped with a number of advanced helmet/sensor systems. Kret

The new Ka-52 forward fuselage section would incorporate the armoured cabin in which the crew of two is seated side-by-side on K-37-800M shock-absorbing ejection seats, part of the 'catapult-cushioning system' which carries the Zvezda index CAS-37-800M. The system is made-up of two main sections, the seat and its associated features that include the ZS-7VS protective helmet and the ECC-BK LP safe emergency escape complex, which incorporates a rocket that effectively tows the escape complex clear of the helicopter at speeds of up to 350 km/h (exceeding the Ka-52 maximum design speed) at altitudes of 0 to 5000 m. The system also reduces the g load effects on the crew through what Zvezda describes as an 'energy absorbing amortization suspension seat' (Zvezda).

As well as providing protection from impacts the ZS-7B(VS) (ZSh-7B) crew helmet, which had been developed by 2001, also incorporates a Sun visor, reduces ambient noise pollution, incorporates an open-channel two-way wireless communication system, a mounting for optical devices such as night vision goggles or sighting apparatus and an oxygen mask, either, a KM-37 or alternatively a KM-32Ar. The RUC-BL-LP system, of which the KM-37 mask is a part, supplies the crew with oxygen at altitudes up to 6000 m, well within the Ka-52 operational parameters (Zvezda).

CAS composition – data furnished by NPP Zvezda

Flight clothing (summer, winter and demi-season); RUC-VK-PL onboard oxygen equipment; ZS-7VS (ZS-7B) helmet, incorporating night vision goggles; to NAZ-il; GMT-5 in water (sea) rescue kit; TSA-74 aircraft rescue belt; with underwater breathing apparatus ADF from the set of rescue equipment KCC

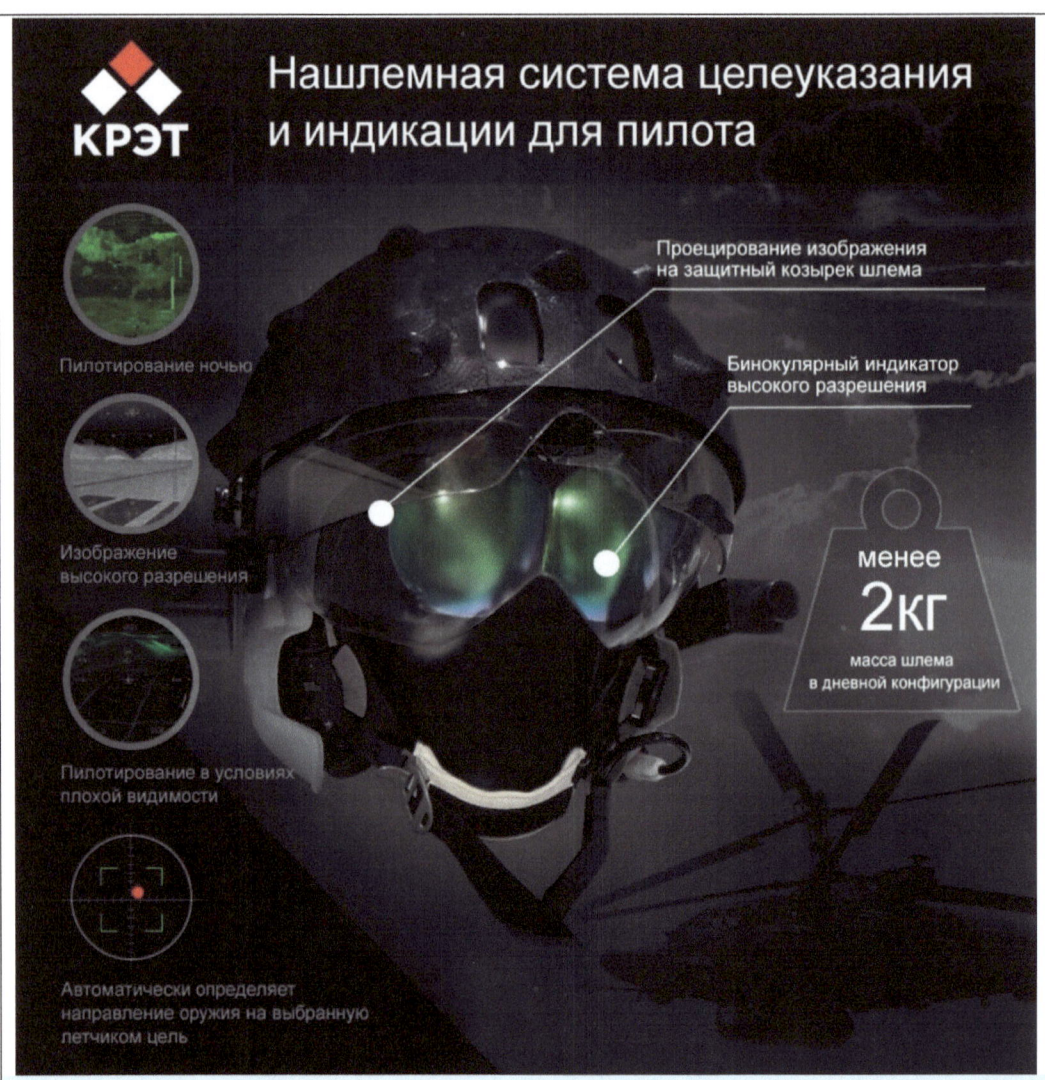

Russian language infographic depicting the HMTDS (Helmet Mounted Targeting Designation System) that is available for the Ka-52. Text is reproduced below with English translation in parenthesis: нашлемная систетма целеуказания и индикации для пилота (System of target designation and indication for the pilot); проецирование изображения на защитный козырек шлема (projecting an image onto a helmet protective cap); бинокулярный индикатор высокого разрешения (high resolution binocular indicator); манее 2кг масса шлема в дневной конфигурации (2 kg weight of helmet in daytime configuration); пилотирование ночью (piloting at night); изображение высокого разрешения (high resolution images); пилотирование в условиях плохой видимости (low visibility piloting). Kret

> CAS specifications – data furnished by NPP Zvezda
>
> **Speed range of operation:** ejection up to 350 km/h
> **Altitude ejection range:** 0-6000 m
> **Weight of equipment for pilot:** 6.5 to 12.8 kg
> **Permissible parameters of occupant from 57.0 to 91.4 kg:** growth of sitting, 810 mm-980 mm
> **Mass of the seat system without pyrotechnic charge:** 57.25 kg

The OVN-1 NVG (Night Vision Goggle) system allows for safer operations in low light conditions, particularly during take-off and landing and low altitude flight operations, providing search and location capabilities in not only night conditions, but in conditions of adverse weather. The NVG incorporate a pair of $2^{nd}+/3^{rd}$ generation bi-planner image intensifying tubes with 18 mm photocathode featuring a great spectral sensitivity. Other features include an automatic adjustment of brightness system that is sensitive to extra-vehicular illumination conditions. The OVN-1 system can be fitted to a number of flight helmet types, including the ZSh-7B employed on the Ka-52.

> OVN-1 Helicopter Pilot Night Vision Goggles
>
> **Field of view:** 38°
> **Magnification power:** 1 x
> **Resolution:** 1.5 millirad
> **Diopter adjustment:** from -5 to +4
> **Interpupillary adjustment:** 53.5-72.7 mm
> **Operating temperature range:** from -40° to +50° C
> **Power supply:** 24-29 V
> **Aircraft electrical system autonomous source:** 2.5-3.5
> **Power consumption:** not more than 3 W
> **Time of continuous operation:** at least 2 hours
> **Weight:** 0.66 kg in working condition
> **Maximum overall dimensions:** 100 x 135 x 90 mm in operating condition

The model of collimator available on the Ka-52 is considered to be either the HUD-31M that equipped the Ka-50 or a derivative. This system is endowed with a wide-field-of-view and incorporates an ILS-31 analogue indicator.

The integrated avionics suite is optimised for all-weather day and night operations including targeting. Much of the airborne equipment complex(s) were developed by RPKB Ramenskoy. This includes the Baguette (Bagett) onboard central computer complex, the BK-77 switching unit for TV (Television) signals, the flight information system, the navigation flight plan complex and the electronic indication system. The aircraft is equipped with an INS-2000 inertial navigation system and an SBKV-2V-2 system for course, heading and vertical changes. The electronic indication system consists of six large format – 38.1 cm (15 in) – MFI-35 multifunction colour active-matrix display screens that replicate various data in high resolution that can be read in all ambient light conditions. The displays feature 40 multifunctional buttons along with a pair of turn dials with integrated buttons. The screen measures an area 304.8 x 228.6 mm. The display features the following functions: 'Video output for the recorder: 1 channel (Fiber Channel); Inputs ARINC-429: 16 listening channels; 1 Fiber Channel; ARINC-429 outputs: 4 outputs; MKIO-1 redundant channel; pilot interface: control panel with dynamically programmable buttons and 2 multi-turn dials with buttons; Software downloadable via the external RS-232 and Ethernet connectors' (RPKB Ramenskoye/Kret).

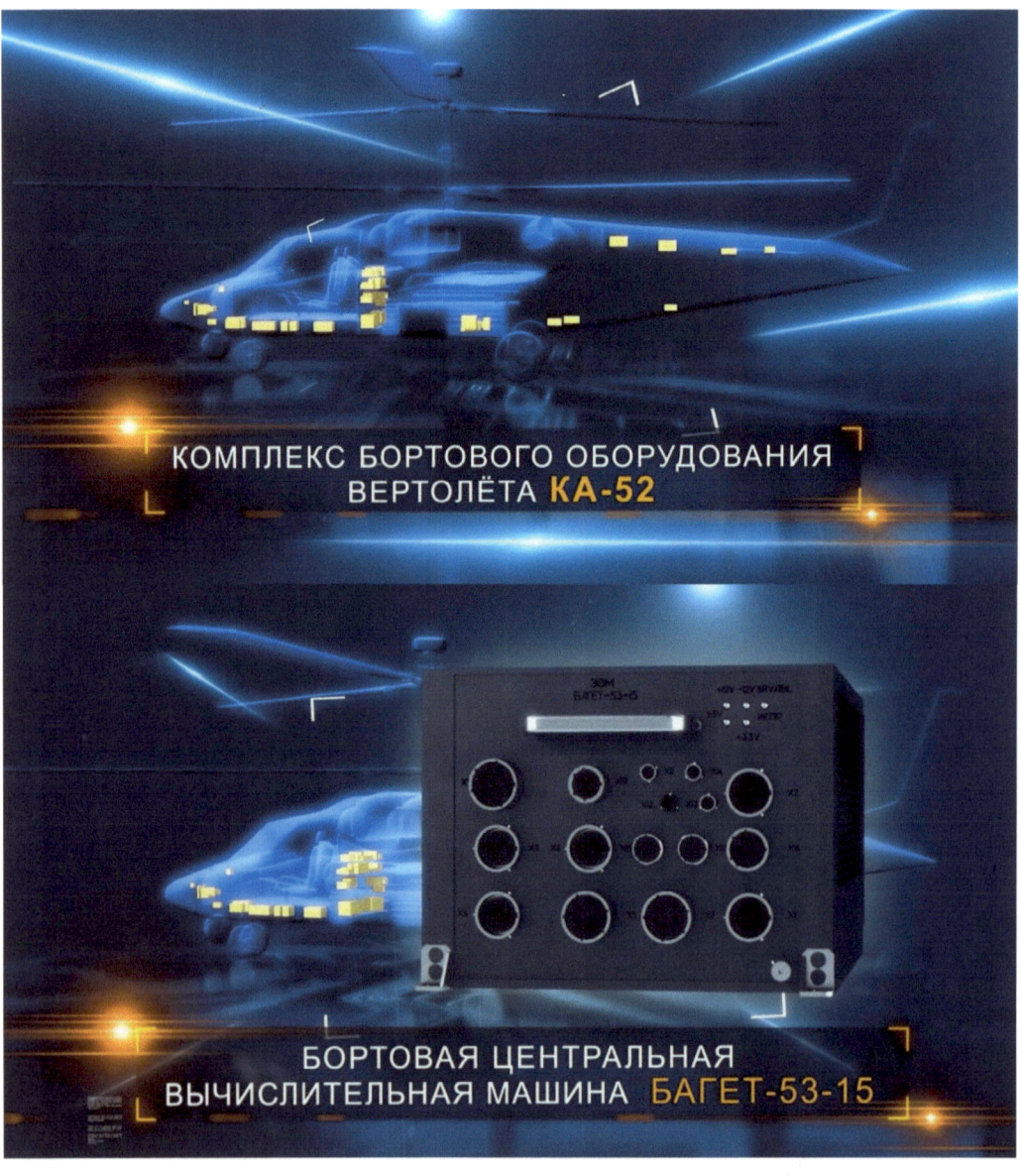

БЛОК КОММУТАЦИИ ТЕЛЕВИЗИОННЫХ СИГНАЛОВ БК-77

ИНЕРЦИАЛЬНАЯ НАВИГАЦИОННАЯ СИСТЕМА ИНС-2000

СИСТЕМА БЕСПЛАТФОРМЕННАЯ КУРСА И ВЕРТИКАЛИ СБКВ-2В-2

СИСТЕМА ЭЛЕКТРОННОЙ ИНДИКАЦИИ

Page 24 top: комплекс бортового оборудования вертолёта (helicopter airborne equipment complex). Page 24 bottom: бортовая центральная вычислительная машина багет-53-15 (onboard central computer Baguette-53-15). Page 25 top: блок коммутации телевизионных сигналов вк-77 (TV signal and switching unit VK-77). Page 25 centre: инерциальная навигационная система инс-2000 (inertial navigation system INS-2000) and система бесплатформенная курса и вертикали сбкв-2в-2 (system of free-of-charge course and vertical SBKV-2V-2). Page 25 bottom: система электронной индикации (electronic indication system). RPKB

This page: Cockpit of a development Ka-52 showing the indication systems and pilots collimator display on the port side. RPKB

MFI-35 characteristics – data furnished by Kret

Dimensions: 270 x 345 x 160 mm
Weight: 12 kg
Consumption from DC network of 27V: 130 W
Consumption of heating circuits from AC 3-phase current 115V Hz: 2S0 VA
Wide viewing angle in landscape orientation: Az = 60° (horizontal); E1 = Gd 0° (in vertical)
High resolution: 1400 x 1050 colour pixels
High contrast
With 1.0 lux ambient light: = 300:1 (at viewing angles Az = 0° E1 = 0°)
With solar illumination (1000, 000 lux): = 10:1 (at viewing angles Az = 0°, E1 = 0°)
Mean time between failures in flight: not less than 7,000 hours

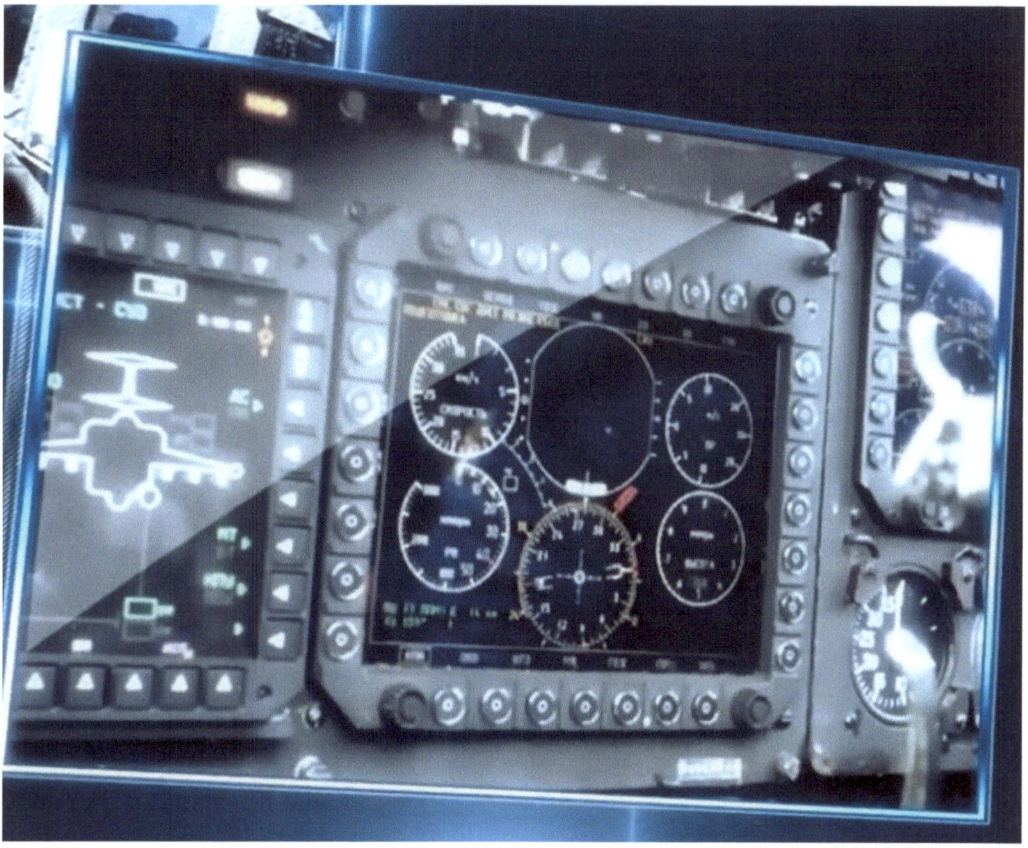

Ка-52/К

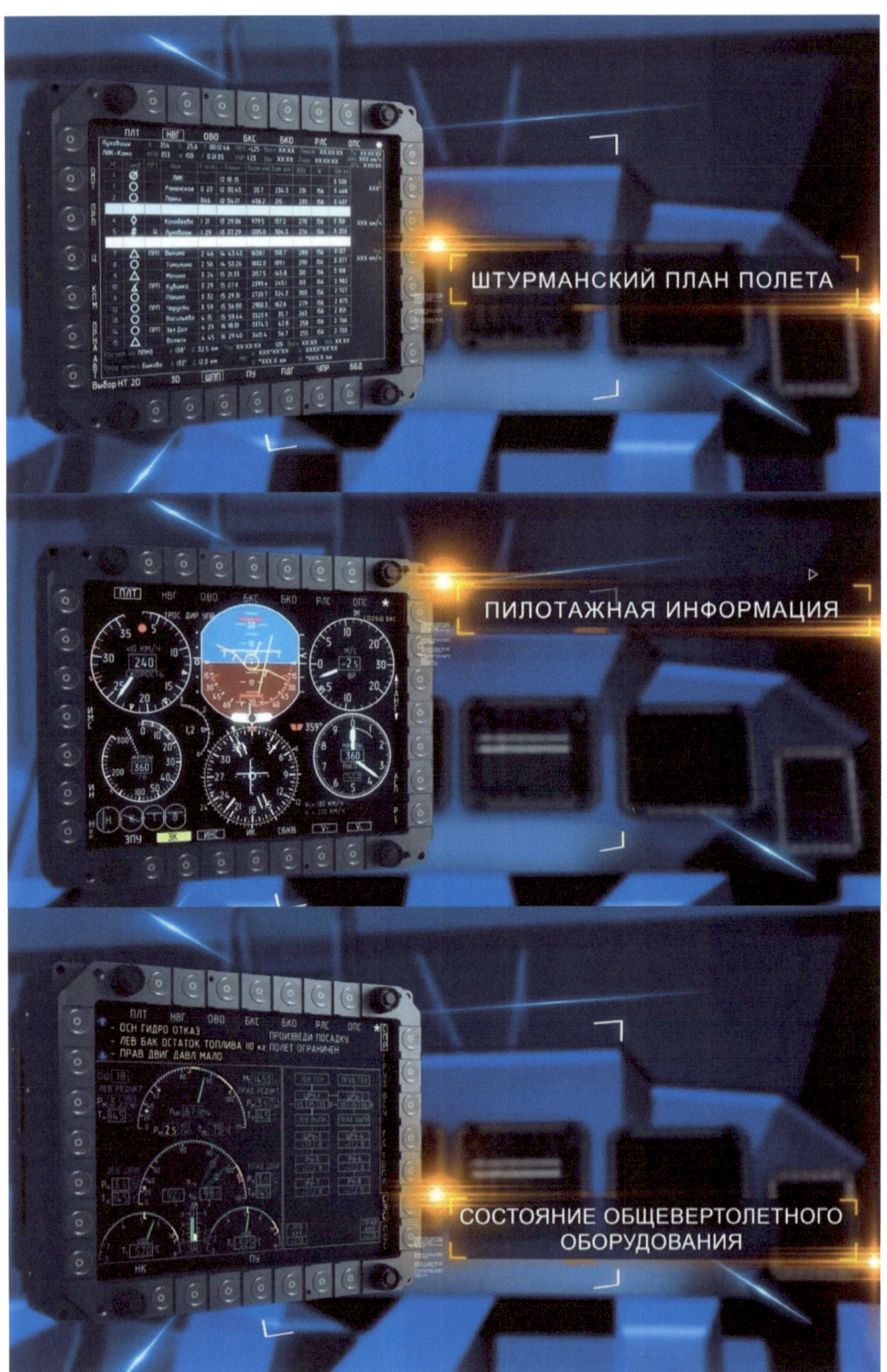

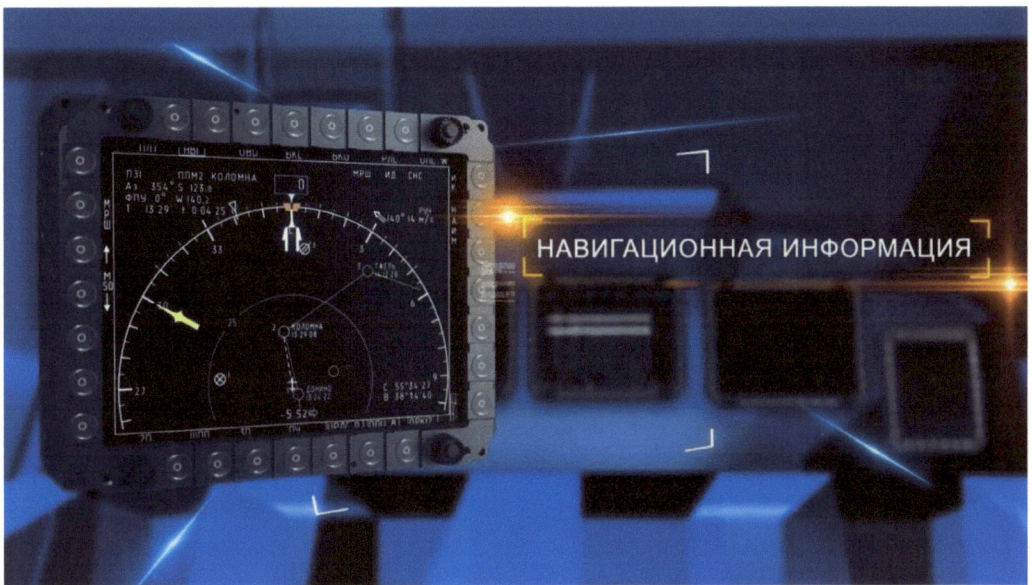

Page 27: The electronic indication system incorporated on the Ka-52/K is centred on six large format multi-function display screens, four of which are visible in the image (top) with the flight information screen (bottom). **Page 28-29:** Russian language graphics depicting the various aviation and display equipment installed in the Ka-52. Text is reproduced below with English translation in parenthesis: штурманский план полета (navigation flight plan); пилотажная информация (flight information); состояние общевертолетного оборудования (state of all helicopter equipment); навигационная информация (navigation information). RPKB

Either of the two pilots would be able to take control of and fly the helicopter at any time during a mission. As well as aircrew protection and combat capability, a high priority in the design of the Ka-52 was the vastly increased levels of automation over legacy systems, including servicing and maintenance diagnostics.

Among the equipment available for incorporation on the Ka-52 is the Ekran-30-52, which is an automated system for control over avionics when the aircraft is in-flight or on the ground. The functions of the system include collecting and conversion of parametric flight information, which is registered and stored in emergency/rescue storage devices; voice recording of crew and storage in emergency device and measures to increase preservation possibility of emergency storage device in the event of the aircraft loss or serious damage. The system enables 'logical processing and preservation of information about failures of systems and components in operation and the timely alert of crews via multifunctional indicators. Interaction with the onboard computer via the GOST 26765.52-87 channel and the transfer of inspection results and the values of the operational sensor with a two-fold redundancy. Preservation of recorded information in the event of an accident in accordance with OST-101080-95 and TSP-C124. Ability to read flight information and overwrite it at the ground surface processing apparatus by the AFK-30 automated functional control device' (Kret).

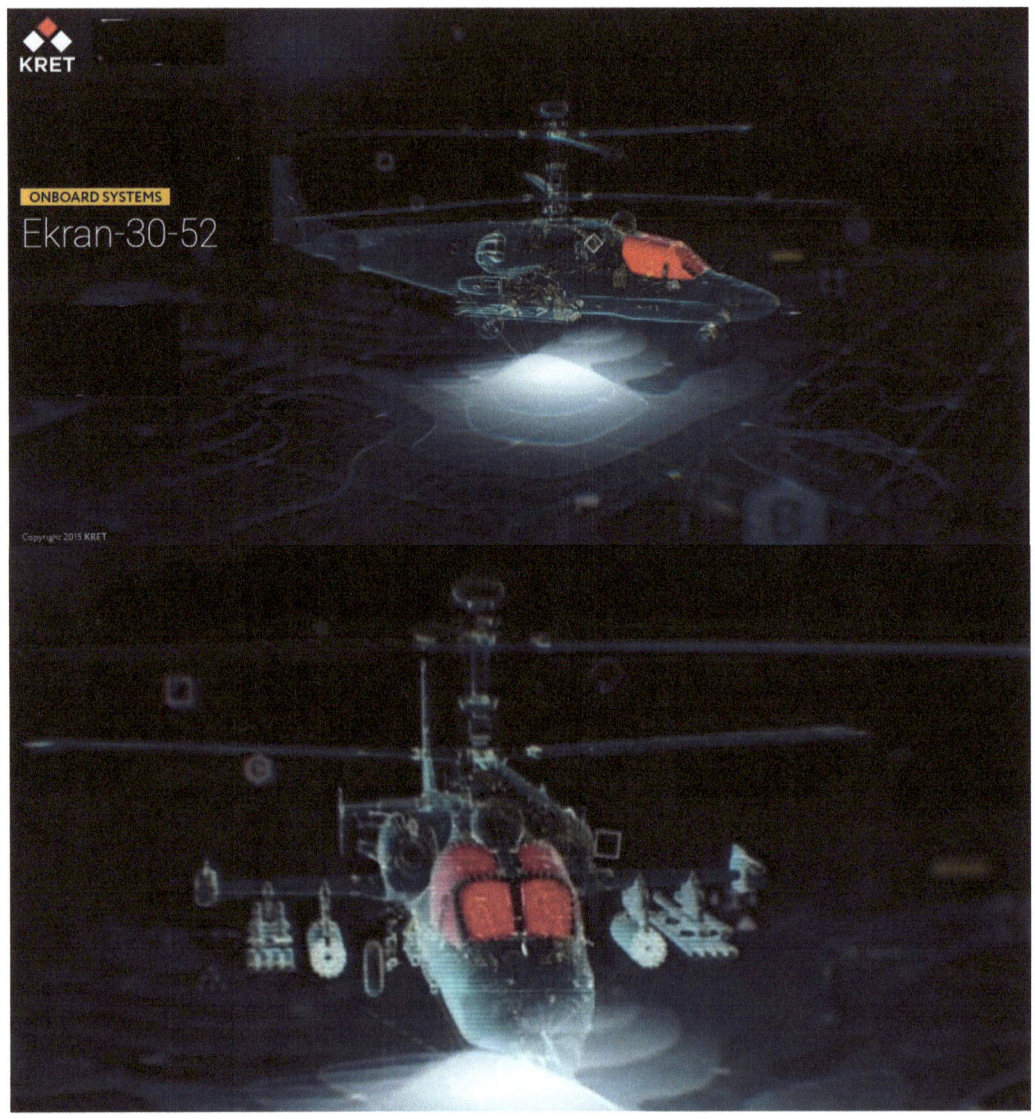

Above: **Ekran-30-52 location on the Ka-52.** Kret

Ekran-30-52

Recording and preservation of information in the last hours; parameter, no less than: 25 hours
Sound (for each of 4 channels), no less than: 2 hours
Number of signals received from the sensors and systems of the aircraft: 93 analog and 168 digital
Serial code GOST 18977-79 and RTM 1495-75: 17
DC supply voltage: 27V
Power consumption: no more than 50 W
Number of reserved channels: not less than 2

Indokraz is a system for the automated preparation of tasking for training of aviation groups. The system, which can be employed by Ka-52, Mi-28N, late Mi-24 and Mi-35M series attack helicopters and fixed wing combat aircraft – Su-27, Su-30MK, Su-35, MiG-29SMT, MiG-29K and MiG-35/D – provides for 'Preparation of electronic maps for onboard indicators. Conversion of action plans for flight tasks and their recordings on Flash-card for entry into the aircraft avionics. Preparation of flight documents. Operation in a circuit of the automated information and flight control according to the principles of network-centric operations. Analysis of single and group flights of aircraft as registered in the flight data' (Kret). It is unclear if this system is operational on Ka-52's in Russian Federation service, but it is available for potential export variants of the Ka-52.

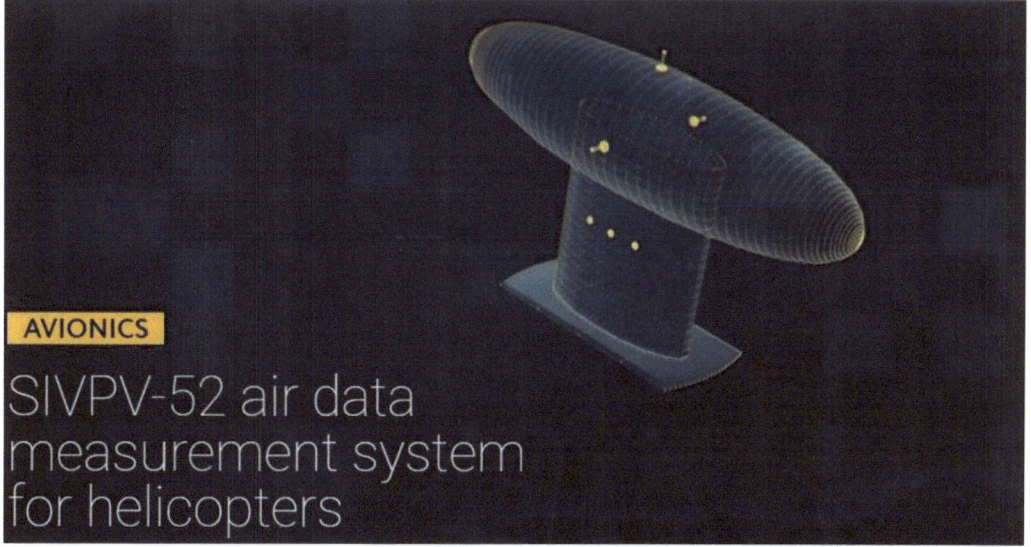

Top: Graphic depicting the SIVPV-52 air data measurement system. Above: Graphic showing the SIVPV positioned on the upper main vertical fin of the Ka-52. Kret

The Ka-52 can be equipped with an SIVPV-52 air data measurement system for helicopters that determines the flight parameters of the helicopter and relays data about all flight modes – forward, backward, pitch (up/down), yaw (sideways), including in near zero airspeed and hovering – to the onboard systems and superimposed on the cockpit display screens. The system is made up of two MIPV modules featuring a streamlined ellipsoidal body. Each of the modules incorporates, as laid down in Kret documentation, 'two pilot static systems (PPS); heating control unit for the PSS; pressure sensor unit; ambient air temperature sensor; calculator for aircraft flight parameters [and a] power source' (Kret). The MIPV receives various data from the helicopter systems, including 'components of the vector of absolute angular velocity relative to the associated axes wC, wU, wZ; vector components of overload associated axes nx, ny, nz; roll, pitch and course angles; current weight of the helicopter mh; pressure at take-off and landing, Pgr; rotor speed [and] geometrical height' (Kret). This system does not appear to be operational on Ka-52's in Russian Federation service, but is available for inclusion on export variants of the helicopter.

The advanced sensor/avionics suite and modern precision guided weapons enable the Ka-52 to be utilised in a variety of combat roles. The main radio electronic sensor system for the Ka-52/K is the day-night/all-weather Arbalet (Crossbow) complex incorporating the Phazotron NIIR FH 01 radar, which completed state joint tests in November 2011. This duel band coherent pulse-Doppler radar is designed to operate in the Ka-band and L-wavelengths through a process of frequency tuning. The system, which was developed as open architecture employing standardised hardware and software modules, incorporates a 'high intelligence computer system' (Kret) and the overall system has no requirement for liquid cooling. A derivative of the Arbalet, designated Arbalet-D was developed for installation in small size ships to allow them to detect and respond to an air attack.

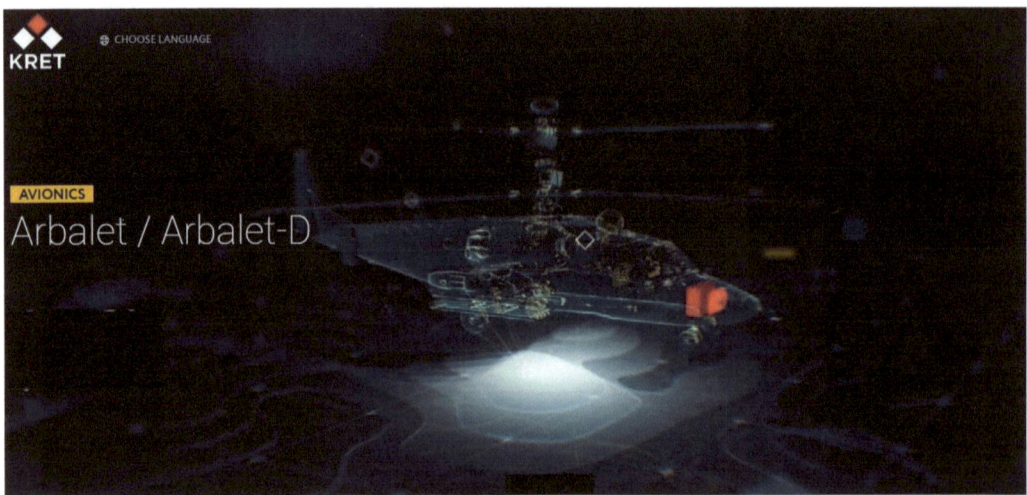

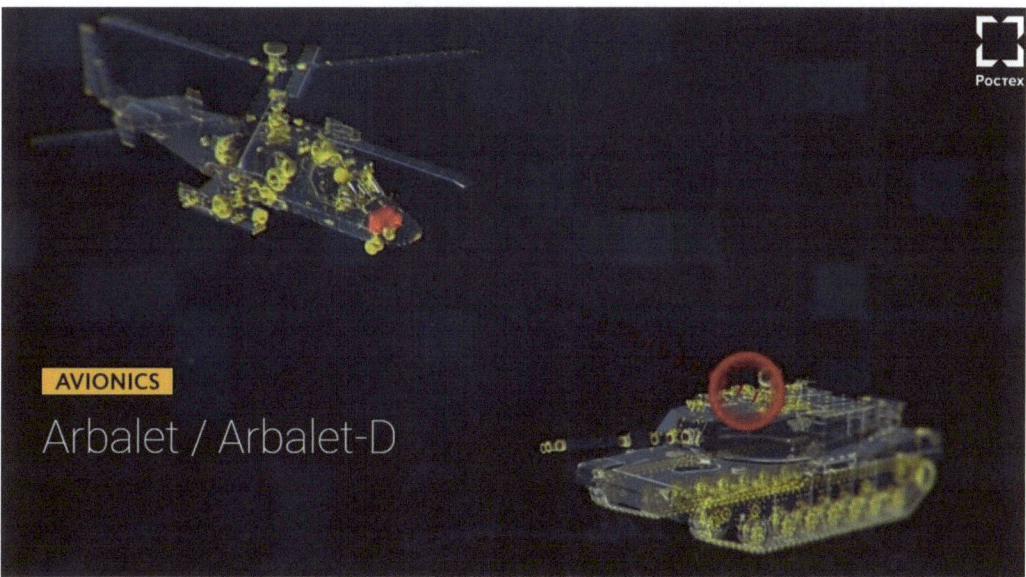

Previous page: Graphic showing the position of the Arbalet main sensor complex located in the nose section of the Ka-52 Alligator. This page: Series of two graphics depicting the targeting of a main battle tank target by the Arbalet complex, anti-armour guided missile launch from a Ka-52 and missile impact on the target. Arbalet also has the ability to launch missiles against slow moving airborne targets such as other helicopters or uninhabited air vehicles Kret/Rostec

Russian language graphic depicting various operating parameters of the Arbalet complex. Kret Text incorporated within the graphic is reproduced below with English translation in parenthesis:

арбалет радиолокационный комплекс (Crossbow radar complex)
всепогодное применение боевых вертолетов (all-weather use of combat helicopters)
дальность обнаружения воздушных целеи: 15 km (range detection of air targets: 15 km)
сопровождает 20 объектов (accompanies [tracks] 20 objects)
дальность обнаружения наземных целеи: 12 km (range detection of ground targets: 12 km)
срок службы 25 лет (service life 25 years)
дальность картографирования 32 km (range of mapping: 32 km)

Ка-52/К

«Арбалет»
Радиолокационный комплекс

Двухдиапазонный когерентно-импульсный радио-локационный комплекс, работающий в Ка и L-диапазонах волн и использующий перестройку частоты.

Построен с использованием унифицированных аппаратных и программных модулей на основе открытой архитектуры. Имеет вычислительную систему высокого интеллекта. Не требует жидкостного охлаждения.

Обеспечивает круглосуточное, всепогодное применение боевых вертолетов.

Режим «воздух-поверхность»

120° Зона обзора по азимуту

32 км Дальность картографирования

Дальность обнаружения наземных целей

 25 км мосты

 12 км танки

Режим «воздух-воздух»

360° Зона обзора по азимуту
угол места: +/-30

0,5 сек Время обнаружения цели типа «Стингер»

Дальность обнаружения воздушных целей

 15 км штурмовики — 5 км «Стингер»

Сопровождает **20** объектов

150 часов Надежность, наработка на отказ на земле и в полете

25 лет Срок службы

5000 часов Ресурс

Russian language graphic providing basic information of the Arbalet complex parameters. Text is reproduced over page 35-36 with English translation in parenthesis: арбалет радиолокационный комплекс (Crossbow radar complex); двухдиапазонный когерентно-импульсный радио-локационный комплекс, работающий в ка и L-диапазонах волн и использующий пюрестройку частоты. построен с использованием унифицированных аппаратных и программных модулей на основе открытой архитектуры. имеет вычислительную систему высокого интеллекта. не требует жидкостного охлаждения. обеспечивает круглосуточное, всепогодное применение боевых вертолетов (a duel-band coherent-pulsed radio-locating complex operating in the Ka and L-bands of waves and using frequency tuning. It is built using unified hardware and software modules based on open architecture. Has a high intelligence computing system. Does not require liquid cooling. Provides round the clock all-weather, use of combat helicopters); сопровождает 20 объектов (accompanies [tracks] 20 objects)

режим воздух-поверхность (air to surface mode)
120° зона обзора (Field of view: 120°)
32 km дальность картографирования (32 km range of mapping)
дальность обнаружения наземных целей (range detection of ground targets): 25 km мосты (25 km, bridges) and 12 km танки (12 km, tanks)
режим воздух-воздух (air to air mode)
360° зона обзора (360° field of view)
по азимуту (azimuth range): угол места ± 30° (elevation angle ± 30°)
время обнаружения цели типа стингер: 0.5 сек (time to detect a target of the stinger [MANPADS] type: 0.5 seconds)
дальность обнаружения воздушных целей (range of detection, air targets) штурмовики: 15 km (attack aircraft: 15 km) and стингер 5 km (stinger [MANPADS ((Man Portable Air Defence Systems)] 5 km)
надежность, наработка на отказ на земле и в полете (reliability, time between failures on land and in flight): 150 часов (150 hours)
25 лет срок службы (25 years-service life)
5000 часов ресурс (5000 hour resource)

The FH 101 duel-band coherent pulsed radar system at the heart of the Arbalet (Crossbow) Radar Fire Control System complex operates in the Ku-band and L-waves and employs frequency tuning. Phazotron NIIR

Crossbow Radar system of the Arbalet complex – Phazotron NIIR

'Arbalet allows the Ka-52 to operate in all-weather day and night against air and surface targets. The system can also detect incoming projectiles such as MANPADS

As outlined by Phazotron NIIR and the parent company Kret, the main functions of the complex include:

Air-to-surface

Mapping the Earth's surface; detection and measurement of coordinates of ground (surface) targets

Selection of moving ground (surface) targets

Ensures the function of 'air-to-air' missiles and on-board gun(s)

Low altitude flight

Detection of ground obstacles

Ensures evasion and flight around ground obstacles

Ensures flight following the terrain

'Air-to-Air'

Detection and measurement of the coordinates of aerial targets

Recognition of aerial targets

Ensures anti-aircraft missile defence

Ensures the function of 'air-to-air' missiles and on-board guns

Meteo [Meteorological]

Identification and assessment of boundaries and danger of meteorological formation' Phazotron NIIR & Kret)

Arbalet Performance Characteristics

Air to surface mode

Field of view in azimuth: 120°

The range of mapping: up to 32 km

Detection range for ground targets: 25 km against a bridge size target and 12 km against a tank size target

Detection range of ground obstacles and for determining the terrain: transmission lines – 0.4 km; terrain with slopes of more than 10° – 1.5 km

Accompanying support: up to 20 targets

Air to air mode

Field of view (detection)
    Azimuth: 360°
    Elevation: ± 30°

Detection range of air targets: 15 km against a fighter aircraft size target and 5 km against a 'Stinger' [MANPADS] size missile target

Time for detection of Stinger missile: 0.5 seconds

Accompanying support: up to 20 targets

Reliability, mean time between failures on the ground and in-flight: 150 hours

Top and above: The large rotating dome beneath the nose of the Ka-52 houses the major sensors of the TEOS complex. A smaller dome structure (on the bottom image) has been observed on the port side of the forward fuselage underside. The exact function of this instrumentation is unclear, but probably relates to data gathering and calibration during development testing. MODRF

The TOES turret swivels in pitch to expose the sensor heads as the mission profile requires such and closes to protect the sensor heads when not required and during the take-off and landing components of a flight. This frontal aspect view of a Ka-52 in flight (top) shows the exposed TOES sensor heads while the image above shows two Ka-52's, the foremost one of which has the TOES sensor heads protected and the aftermost one with the TOES sensor heads exposed. Rostec/Russian Helicopters

Other systems installed on the Ka-52 include the SYWPV-52 for automatic data recording, the SAU-800 automatic control system – autopilot, Samshit-BM-1 day and night inter-service aiming system and the TOES pilot turret optical-electronic system, which was developed from the GOES-520 (Gyro Stabilised Optoelectronic Station) that is capable of day and night 'ground reconnoiter and ground reference detection' (Rostec Corporation).

A TOES optical-electronic turret, developed from the GOES-520, is positioned on the Ka-52 forward fuselage underside. Kret

The Ka-52 is equipped with 'signature control devices as well as electronic and active counter-measures' for self-defence (Rostec). At the heart of the self-defence protection suite is the President-S ODS (Onboard Defence System), the main function of which is to protect the host aircraft (helicopter) against radar homing surface to air and air to air missiles, airborne launched IR (infrared) guided missiles and Man Portable Air Defence Systems. The President-S complex, which can be carried on various platforms, including tactical combat aircraft, incorporates a laser illumination detector, an ultraviolet missile approach warning system, an electro-optical electronic warfare system and a suite of decoy flares overseen by a central automated control system. The various modular units of the complex can be accommodated within or outside (attached on external structures) the structure of the host platform (Rostec).

In Russian military doctrine the infrared countermeasures of the detachable flare type are considered obsolete. This is attributed to the fact that modern IR homing weapons, be it MANPADS or air launched IR/IIR homing air to air missiles have sensors that are sensitive enough to discriminate between the flare decoy signature and the IR signature of a fast receding aircraft target that clearly stands out amongst the extremely slow speed (which, to modern IR guidance systems appear more or less stationary) and fast reducing in altitude flare decoys. To overcome the lack of protection afforded by the detachable flare systems, the Scientific Research and Development Institute Ekran (USUE NII Ekran) embarked upon an advanced research program (other organisations were involved in such research programs, including Zenit) to determine a new way of defeating IR guided missiles. Eventually it was settled on the idea of using a 'highly-directional pinpoint laser', the function of which would be controlled by an advanced missile launch detection/warning system (Rostec). Whereas single-band (monochromatic) were the international norm, Ekran adopted a multi-spectrum laser emitter that would feature a library of all light spectrums of all known IR/IIR homing heads in use from the first IR guided missiles of the 1950's to the most modern twenty first century weapons of the RVV-BD, AIM-9X, ASRAAM, IRIS-T and modern MANPADS systems. Once a missile threat has been detected the energy from an encoded multi-band laser is precisely directed at the guidance seeker head of the incoming threat missile, the interference resulting in the missile being directed away from the President-S host platform. In effect, a ghost (virtual-reality) target is created within the guidance system of the incoming missile, which homes on this as its new primary target and the warhead detonates some distance from the President-S host platform. The laser countermeasures suite, which incorporates a solid-state laser, 'a single transmitter optical-mechanical module, a control module and a power source', weighs 64 kg (Rostec). This system, which has a coverage of 360° in bearing and 90° in elevation, can counter two IR/IIR guided missiles homing on the host platform simultaneously. The system identifies the type of threat missile(s) involved and tracks same whilst directing the laser beam at the homing head, recoding the exact instant of homing failure in order that attention can be diverted to other threats.

The President-S complex incorporates an active radar countermeasures generator, the function of which is to jam enemy search/tracking and homing radar systems in order to counter radar-guided air to air and surface to air missiles threats For this, 'the system extensively employs radar signal digital processing methods, generating radio noise countermeasures' (Rostec). A host of signal processing and countermeasure techniques DRFM (Digital Radio Frequency Memory) contributes to the provision of protection being provided in complex operational environments such as when the host platform is being threatened by several search/tracking and homing radar systems simultaneously. The active RF (Radio Frequency) jammer effectively jams the tracking/homing radar of the attacking missile(s) at multiple stages of the engagement – detection, tracking and terminal homing. The complex is entirely automated, the crew simply being informed of the direction and trajectory angle that a threat missile is approaching from as well as what countermeasures have been deployed to counter the threat and the status of remaining countermeasures available.

Following tests of early development examples a production variant was manufactured for testing in 2009. In operational combat scenario testing a number of MANPADS missiles were launched at a single helicopter protected by President-S, all of the incoming weapons being effectively defeated. The initial development of the complex was competed in 2015, paving the way for operational deployment on a number of platforms, including the Ka-52 (Rostec).

Sensor element of the President-S complex. Rostec

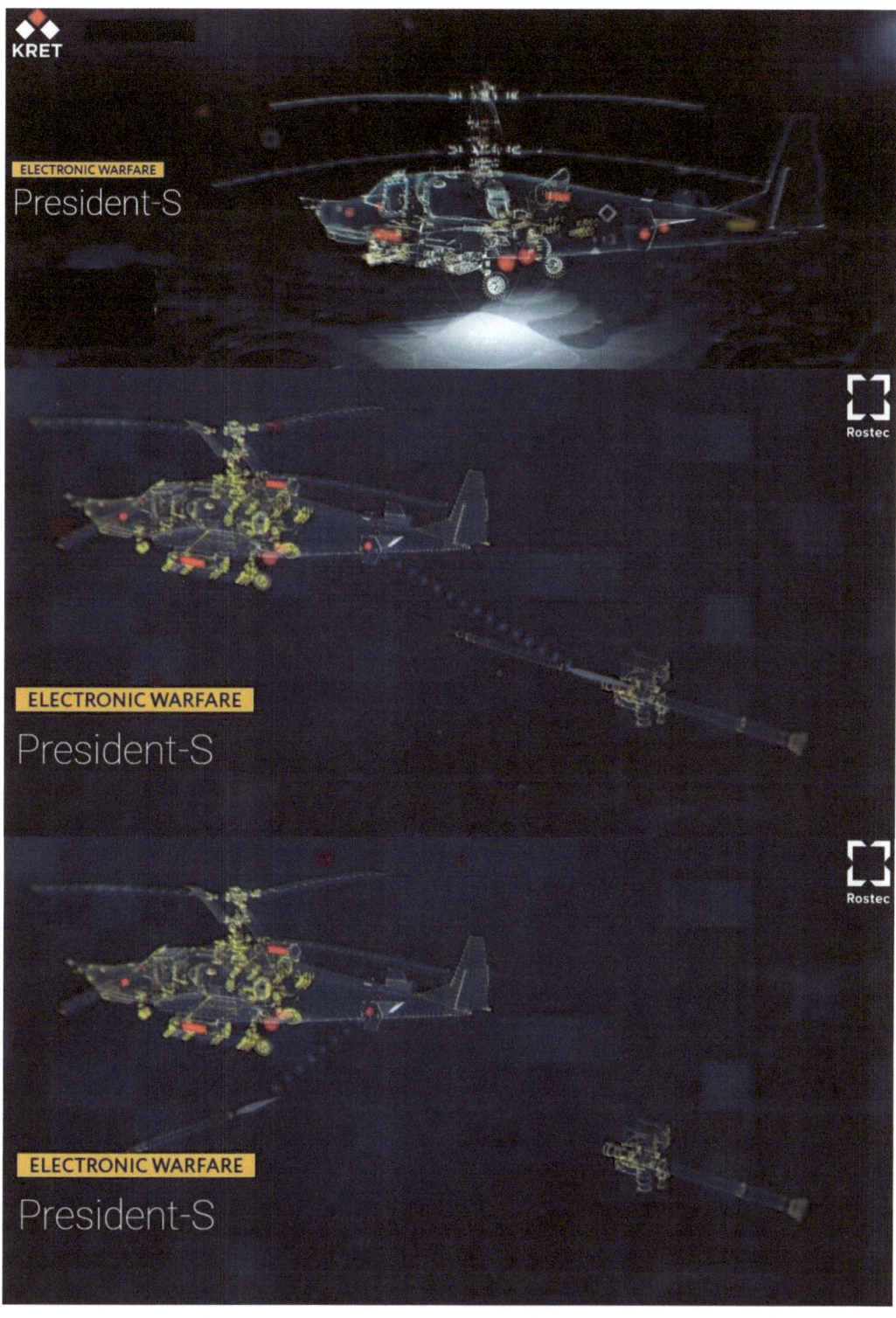

Top: Graphic showing the various locations of the President-S components on the Ka-52. Centre and above: Two graphics depicting the President-S complex being targeted by and diverting away a MANPADS type missile. Kret/Rostec

Graphic depicting the employment of the Vitebsk Electronic Warfare complex. Kret

Another element available for the Ka-52 protection suit is a system referred to as the Vitebsk Electronic Warfare complex. Vitebsk is designed to protect the host platform from a range of threats, including missiles equipped with semi-active or active radar guided homing heads and missiles equipped with Infrared guided homing heads. The system can be deployed on ground based platforms, fast jet airborne platforms and helicopters such as the Ka-52, Mil-28N/UB attack helicopter, Mi-8AMTSh assault transport helicopter, Mi-26T heavy lift transport helicopters and is planned for integration on large transport aircraft of the Ilyushin Il-76MD-90A variant. It is unclear if this system is incorporated on Ka-52's in Russian Federation service.

Ka-52's carrying long range external fuel tanks (top) and anti-tank guided missiles (above). Russian Helicopters/Rosoboronexport

Ka-52's configured with various stores options. Russian Helicopters

Ка-52К катран (Katran) - Full scale development of the Ka-52K, a variant of the Ka-52 'Alligator' scout/attack helicopter optimised for shipboard/maritime operations, commenced in 2012. In line with its maritime role the Ka-52K was designed with a number of naval specific traits, such as folding rotor blades, folding wings, a strengthened undercarriage system, the incorporation of various naval specific systems and the application of a robust anti-corrosion protection coating. As noted above, this variant is thought to, perhaps, have the potential for integration of long-range anti-ship cruise missiles of the Kh-35E type. While no official information has been released to support this assessment, Russian Helicopters confirmed that the new folding wing has also been 'upgraded for the installation of heavy weapons' (Russian Helicopters). As well as aircrew protection and combat capability, a high priority in design of the Ka-52K was the vastly increased levels of automation, including servicing and maintenance diagnostics, over legacy systems.

Previous page: Port side profile view diagram of the Ka-52K. Previous page bottom: Russian language graphic that translates to provide the basic physical and performance specifications and detail armament options for the Ka-52K. Above: The Ka-52K, shown in model form, features folding wings and rotor blades and extensive anti-corrosion protection. MODRF/Rostec Corporation

The folding mechanisms allow the required storage space for each Ka-52K to be reduced, allowing more aircraft to be stored or additional workspace for aircraft to be maintained and armed within the confines of a ships hanger. The incorporation of extensive corrosion resistant materials into the construction was necessitated by the maritime nature of the Ka-52K mission. As was the case with the land based Ka-52, fueling the Ka-52K is accomplished through a single-point refueling system. The Ka-52K also features an upgraded air conditioning system to facilitate the ventilation of the maritime rescue suits for the crew (Russian Helicopters). Additional electronics equipment that the Ka-52K is equipped with, lacking on the land based Ka-52, includes a short-range radio-technical navigation system and the ARK (Air Rescue Kit) that includes maritime specific rescue equipment. It has been suggested, but no conclusive confirmation has been forthcoming as of early 2018, that the TOES complex of the Ka-52 is substituted by a complex designated GOES-451 in the Ka-52K. It has also been noted that the Ka-52K is currently the only naval specific helicopter equipped with an ejection system - the same system as installed on the land based Ka-52 (Russian Helicopters).

The Ka-52K prototype conducted its maiden flight at the Progress Aviation flight test facility on 7 March 2015 crewed by JSC Kamov test pilot Nail Azin and navigator Alexander Sheivkin. As of late 2017, four prototype and development Ka-52K's had been built (Russian Helicopters). Two of these aircraft were allocated to the air group of the Russian Federation Navy Aircraft Carrying Heavy Cruiser, *Admiral of the Fleet of the Soviet Union, Kuznetsov,* which was deployed to the Eastern Mediterranean Sea from late 2016 through February 2017 to support Russian military efforts that were supporting the Syrian Arab Republics fight against ISIS (Islamic State) and other opposition groups that had taken over much of Syria's land mass. This combat deployment was conducted under the auspices of the Ka-52K test program. Although, at the time of writing, there is no released breakdown for the number or types of operational sorties flown by the Ka-52K in Syria, it has been stated by the MODRF and Russian Helicopters that the Ka-52K (design) successfully carried out all missions allocated to it. On the return from the Mediterranean in early March 2017, the Kamov Design Bureau conducted a study program before the test team embarked upon additional test phases with the two helicopters, which was completed the day prior to participation in the 2017 Navy Day Parade. Among the activities in this new phase was interaction testing of the various shipborne systems, including the shipboard navigation system, during take-off and landing operations – a series of seven landings being conducted aboard the newly commissioned Russian Federation Navy Frigate *Admiral Gorshkov.* While the testing aboard the *Admiral Gorshkov* may have been suggestive of an intention to operate Ka-52K helicopters from such vessels, the more likely explanation was that this vessel was equipped with new generation systems of the type that would be expected to be incorporated into the planned Russian designed and built Helicopter Carrier(s) that the Russian Navy hopes to acquire in place of the cancelled Mistral Class. It would, of course, be possible to operate a Ka-52K from a Frigate class of warship, but this is unlikely to become commonplace as it would be at the expense of the ASW (Anti-Submarine Warfare) helicopters carried on this class of warship.

A fleet of four Mistral Class Helicopter Carriers had been planned for long term acquisition by the Russian Federation Navy. However, if a domestic replacement for Mistral is indeed acquired, the build program may be scaled back. Assuming that up to three of the Mistrals – each with eight Ka-52K - would have been expected to be operational at any one time, this would suggest a minimum planned operational fleet of 24 Ka-52K's, not taking into account the requirement for shore based training and continuation development trials, which would have extended the fleet.

Amphibious landing capability, as had been the case with the Soviet Union during World War II and the Cold War decades, remains an important element of the Russian Federations active defence doctrine. This is required not so much to project power to distant shores, but to support peripheral operations by the Russian Army along the coasts of the Baltic and Black seas in the event of hostilities with NATO. During the later Cold War years and in the early 1990's, NATO was highly conscious of such Soviet/Russian capabilities to employ amphibious/heli-borne assault warfare in peripheral support operations on the Central and Southern European fronts. Consequently, NATO doctrine included extensive training to counter such operations, an operational training element largely, if not completely lacking in NATO armies in the twenty first century.

Above: Concept model of a Russian designed helicopter carrier to replace the Mistral Class helicopter carriers ordered from France, but cancelled following the imposition of European Union sanctions on Russia in 2014. The carrier concept is shown with Kamov (Russian Helicopters) Ka-29 assault transport and Ka-52K naval attack helicopters. Kret

Prior to the availability of the Ka-52K prototype, which conducted its maiden flight at the Progress Aviation flight test facility on 7 March 2015, Ka-52's were involved in various facets of developing the maritime variant. A Ka-52 is here on the approach to land on a Russian naval vessel. Russian Helicopters

In one such large-scale NATO military exercise that took place more decades past than this writer, then serving in an infantry unit of the Argyll and Sutherland Highlanders, cares to admit to, said unit was tasked to defend, against a heli-borne assault force, a windswept stretch of coast near the small ferry town of Oban on the Scottish West coast. The Highlanders had landed at the remote coastal location the previous evening, courtesy of a RAF Boeing Chinook HC.1 transport helicopter, and immediately dug in according to operational doctrine then in force. Just after dawn the following morning the position was assaulted by a force of Royal Marines carried in a quartet of RAF Westland Puma HC.1 transport helicopters, simulating, presumably Mi-8 or Ka-29 assault helicopters (unarmed), dressed up with Red Stars for the occasion. The exercise umpires, through visual and sensor means, decreed that the Highlanders (Company strength on paper, although it barely consisted of platoon strength in actuality) had destroyed two of the helicopters on the approach to land and a third on landing – all courtesy of intense small arms fire and 84 mm Carl Gustav shoulder launched infantry anti-tank rocket launchers. This left only the troops delivered in the fourth helicopter as active for the ground assault, which never really got beyond the start phase as the resultant firefight was decreed over, in the Highlanders favour, in under one minute, such was the intensity of overlapping L1A1 SLR rifle, LMG and GPMG 7.62 mm calibre machine gun fire. What the above training exercise had clearly shown was that an opposed (by well trained and disciplined infantry) landing by assault helicopters, without the aid of other assets such as attack helicopters to suppress ground defence positions, could only be conducted at very high cost and would, unless overwhelming numbers were involved, result in abject failure. The Americans had learnt this bitter lesson during the Vietnam War in the 1960's and early 1970's and the Soviets learned same during their experience in Afghanistan in 1979-88. Such ground force suppression operations are one of the major tasks that would be allotted to the Ka-52K, which is a quantum leap in capability over the support afforded by the Ka-29 armed assault helicopter – which would be nullified when the helicopter was landing its cargo.

Ka-52/K Alligator/Katran – data furnished by Russian Helicopters, Rosoboronexport and the MODRF

Maximum take-off weight: 10800 kg
Normal take-off weight: 10400 kg (conflicting Russian Helicopters documentation states 10400 kg as the maximum take-off weight). Russian Helicopters data suggests a take-off weight of up to 12200 kg for the Ka-52K
Engines: 2 x TGN Klimov TV3-117VMA turboshaft, each rated at 2400 hp. or VK-2500/VK-2500P turboshaft, each rated at 2400 hp. (Klimov documentation suggests a rating of ~1660 kW (2200 hp.) at take-off)
Length (with rotors): 15.86 m
Fuselage length: 13.9 m
Rotor diameter: 14.5 m
Width (with landing gear): 4.611 m
Wing span: 6.3 m
Wing span in folded position: 4.3 m (Ka-52K)
Height (in storage): 5.01 m
Static ceiling (hovering): Up to 4000 m (Russian Helicopters data suggests a reduction to 3600 m for the Ka-52K)
Operational ceiling: 5500 m (Russian Helicopters data suggests a reduction to 5200 m for the Ka-52K)
Maximum acceleration at sea level: 16 m/s
Vertical acceleration at sea level: 12 m/s (Russian Helicopters data states 16 m/s)
Maximum speed: 300 km/h (MODRF documentation states 310 km/h for TV3-117VMA powered variant). Russian Helicopters data suggests that the maximum speed is reduced to 290 km/h for the Ka-52K
Cruising speed: 260 km/h (Russian Helicopters data suggests this may be reduced to 250 km/h for the Ka-52K)
Maximum speed in yaw flight: 80 km/h
Maximum speed in backwards flight: 90 km/h (MODRF documentation suggests a backward speed of 100 mph (160 km/h), but this is considered erroneous)
Ferry range: 1100 km (MODRF states 1160 km as a practical ferry range)
Practical range (internal fuel tanks): 460 km (the Ka-52K is stated to have a practical range of 450 km on internal fuel)
Maximum payload: 2500 kg (Russian Helicopters states 2000 kg for the Ka-52K)
Armament: 1 x 30 mm 2A42 automatic cannon with 460 rounds (conflicting documentation states 500 rounds, but this is considered to be erroneous) of 30 mm ammunition and a diversity of munitions, which can include various mixes of 4 x 20 launchers for C-80FP 80 mm or 4 x 5 launchers for C-13 122 mm rockets; 2 x 6 launchers for Ataka anti-armour missiles or 2 x 6 launchers with Whirlwind, Shturm-VU ATGM, an unstated number of Hermes-A general purpose air to surface missiles or launchers for 4 x Igla air to air guided missiles. The C-13, Hermes or Igla does not form part of the armament options available to Ka-52's in Russian service in 2018
Crew: 2

Ka-52 helicopters of the Russian Aerospace Forces. MODRF

Top: Ka-52 operating with the Russian Eastern Military District. Above: A Ka-52 operating with the Russian Southern Military District. MODRF

Ka-52's during overwater testing, including in surface effect hover tests (above).
Russian Helicopters

Further development continues of various systems for future application on land and maritime based variants of the Ka-52. As an example, the Russian Space Corporation, 'Roscosmos', is involved in development of a new, as yet unspecified, system that will enhance the ability of the Ka-52 to strike ground targets (RCC). A number of other institutions and corporations continue developments of enhancements to existing systems and or development of new systems that could find future application on Russia's new generation scout/attack helicopter designs.

Ka-52's in service with the Russian Federation Aerospace Forces. MODRF

3

KA-52/K WEAPONS COMPLEX

The Ka-52/K in Russian Federation service are cleared for operations with a diversity of air to surface and mixed air to air/air to surface precision guided and unguided weapon systems that can effectively be used against a diversity of armoured and soft-skinned surface and airborne target sets. The operation of airborne armament is overseen by the SUO-806P WCSH (Weapons Control Systems for Helicopters). This comprises the 'integrated controller for autonomous operation life; units for the conversion of interfaces with weapons; peripheral units for interfacing with weapon [and] redundant control panels' (Kret). At the heart of the WCSH is a multi-processor control system employing solid-state switching technology. Incorporated in the system is the built-in monitoring capability to scan the component status and provide an interface with weapon systems (Kret). The Aviaavtomatika stores management system provides direct control over the deployment of guided and unguided stores. This system comprises the autonomous operation integrated controller and conversion system for the coupling of stores interface incorporated within the system of management for peripheral stores coupling.

The Ka-52 fixed armament, as was the case for the Ka-50, would consist of the NPPU-80 2A42-1 30 mm rapid fire gun unit that is capable of automatic and single shot firing, the Ka-52 having the capacity to accommodate 460 30 mm rounds. This weapon, which is also incorporated in the Mi-28N attack helicopter and a number of armoured vehicles – BMD-2, BMD-3 tracked infantry fighting vehicles, BTR-90 wheeled armoured personnel carrier and the BMPT tank assistance combat vehicle – employs a single-barrel gas operated action system to achieve high reliability in operation. A fixed receiver aids the ammunition belt feed, the ammunition being used up in a process of selective feeding, with alteration of firing rates. Extended close range (point-blank) firing is aided by the guns long-barrel design with significant enhancements to overall accuracy facilitated by the muzzle brake system and shock absorption of the recoiling barrel. This provides a steady firing platform by reducing oscillation of the mount at the exact instant each round is discharged.

The Ka-52 design features six stations for external stores carriage – three on each of the wings. The cannon armament is mounted in a recessed station on the starboard side lower fuselage. MODRF/Kret

Top: Graphic showing the locations of the WCSH modules on the Ka-52. Above: NPPU-80 2A42 30 mm rapid fire gun. Kret/Splav

NPPU-80 2A42 30 mm rapid fire gun unit - data furnished by Tulamashzavod Production Association

Round type: GSh-6-30
Caliber: 30 mm
Weight of gun: 115 kg
Length of gun: 3027 mm
Rate of fire
    High: 550-800 rounds per minute
    Low: 200-300 rounds per minute
Muzzle velocity: 960 m/s
Practicable range: up to 1500 m against lightly armoured targets and up to 4000 m against soft skinned targets and personnel
Recoil force: 40-50 kN (4000-5000 kgf)
DC power supply voltage of electric trigger and contractor: 27V
Gun ammunition feed: two-belt
Charging: pyrotechnic and manual
Firing control: remote from electric trigger and mechanical
Operating temperatures: ±50° C

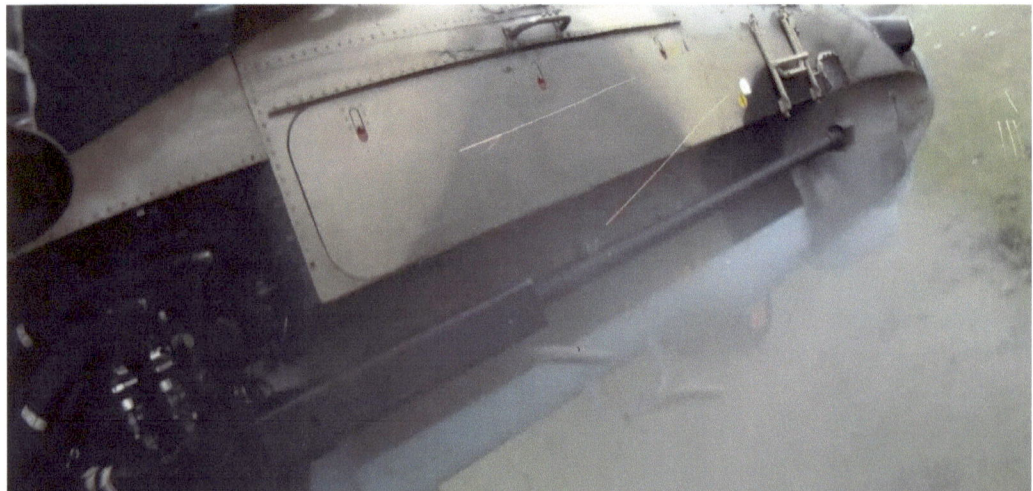

Three still sequence of the operation of the Ka-52 2A42-1 30 mm rapid fire gun.
MODRF

The Vikhr-1 ATGM/AAM system is the primary anti-tank guided missile/air to air missile system employed on the Russian Aerospace Forces Ka-52. Rostec

The Ka-52 primary guided missile armament consist of the Strelets missile system. Launch systems are incorporated for guided missiles including Ataka and Vikhr-1 (twelve missiles accommodated) 'Whirlwind' ATGM (Anti-Tank Guided Missile). The Vikhr-1, developed by KBP instrument Design Bureau, was initially accepted for service with the armed forces of the Soviet Union in 1982. In the 1990's, work commenced on development of the missile for operation with the Ka-50 attack helicopter and the Su-25TM attack aircraft. Vikhr-1, deployed as part of the Vikhr-M 9K12M ATGM complex, is designed to engage and destroy heavily armoured MBT (Main Battle Tank), including such systems that are protected by active armour. The missile, which can be launched to ranges out to 10 km from altitudes up to 4 km, cruises to the target at high supersonic speed – 610 m/s (2196 km/h).

The Vikhr-1, in addition to being the primary anti-tank guided missile, is also the primary air to air missile system employed on the Russian Aerospace Forces Ka-52 and Ka-50 attack helicopters – there being no provision for carriage of the air to air derivative of the Igla MANPADS (Man Portable Air Defence System). Vikhr-1 can be employed against airborne targets flying at speeds up to 800 km/h. The missiles high supersonic speed facilitates a short flight time, reducing exposure to enemy countermeasures, the kinetic energy and warhead combination making it possible to destroy several targets with a single missile, assuming close proximity.

A contract for new generation Vikhr-1 missiles for the MODRF (Ministry of Defence of the Russian Federation) was placed with Izmash, a Kalashnikov Concern company, in July 2013, a batch of test missiles being delivered towards the end of that year. These missiles were used in a test program that was conducted in late 2013 through early 2014. The first batch of operational missiles was delivered to the MODRF from October 2015. The delivery schedule for the MODRF contract was scheduled to continue through 2016, in which year further MODRF contracts, for delivery of additional missile batches, were announced, along with a contract to supply Vikhr-1 to an undisclosed export customer.

The SHTURM-VU air to surface/air to air missile has been specified for the Ka-52. KBM

SHTURM-VU Air to Surface/Air to Air Guided Missile System – Another guided weapon specified for the Ka-52 is the SHTURM-VU multi-channel laser beam riding missile system that can be employed against a number of air to surface target sets and can also be deployed against slow moving airborne targets such as helicopters. The missile complex, which can be operated in adverse weather conditions 24 hours a day, is centred around the 9M120-1 missile armed with a tandem HEAT (High Explosive Anti-Tank) warhead and the 9M120-1F armed with a HE (High Explosive) warhead. Other elements of the complex include a radio command system, ballistic computer and the all-weather, day-night surveillance and targeting system that includes a laser guidance unit, and a processing system for video imagery, incorporating the OKHTNIK ('Hunter') automated TV (Television) tracker system. This complex is integrated with the Ka-52 cockpit display screens, the helicopter fire control system and the helicopter weapon launchers (KBM).

Missiles in the class of Vikhr-1 and SHTURM-VU bestow upon the Ka-52 the ability to engage a multitude of surface targets and slow moving airborne targets such as other helicopters. MODRF/Russian Helicopters

Data from KBM documentation indicates that the SHTURM-VU has a 2000 m longer effective launch range in daylight than the SHTURM-VK system, incorporating the Ataka missile, arming the Mi-35M assault/transport helicopter.

> SHTURM-VU – data furnished by KBM
>
> **Minimum launch range:** 1000 m
> **Maximum effective launch range:** 6000 m in daylight and 3500-4000 m in nighttime conditions
> **Control system:** semi-automatic multi-channel, remote orientation laser-beam riding

9M120 (9M120F) Ataka (Attack) – The Ataka missile is armed with a tandem or retractable warhead capable of destroying all armoured vehicles from MBT to IFV (Infantry Fighting Vehicle), even in the face of 'protective screen dynamic protection'. The warhead is capable of penetrating normal/homogenous armour up to 800 mm in thickness. The 9.5 kg TNT equivalent warhead allows the missile to be used against other targets, such as fortifications in which the explosive power can be used to suppress enemy counter fire during an assault.

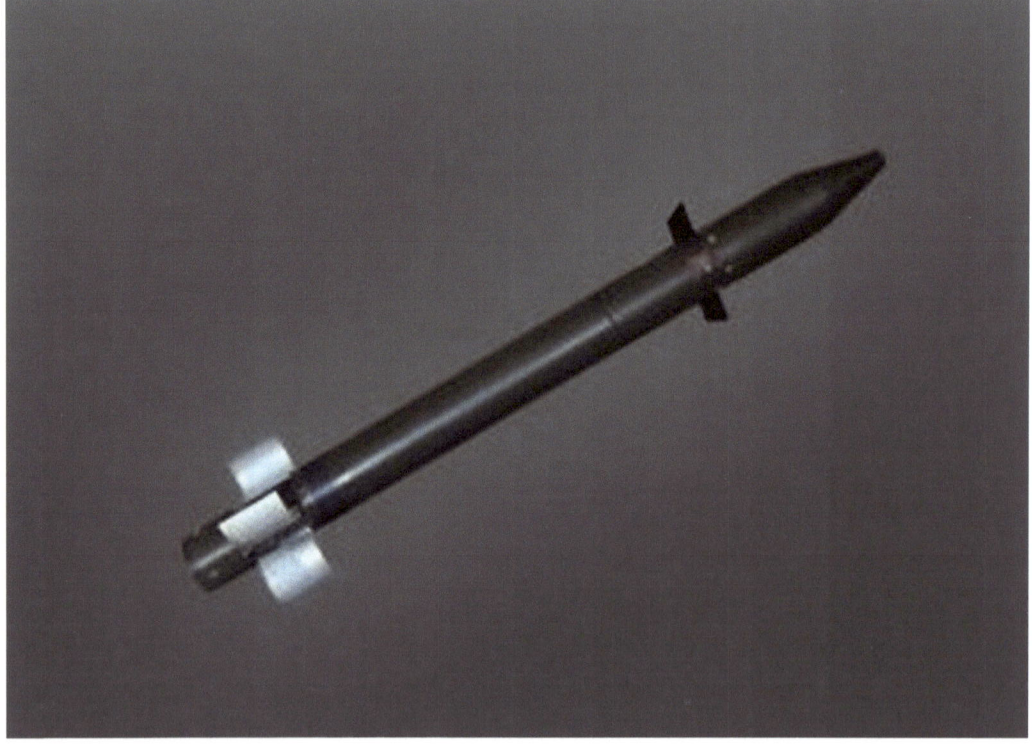

Graphic depiction of the 9M120F, similar to the 9M120-1F specified for the Ka-52. OJSC Degtyareva

Ataka missiles carried on stub stations of a Mi.28N attack helicopter. KBM

> 9M120 (9M120F) Ataka – data, furnished by OJSC Plant VA Degtyareva, specified only for Mi-28N, Mi-24V, Mi-8AMTSh and 9P149 combat vehicle
>
> **Caliber:** 130 mm
> **Length:** 1830 mm
> **Mass:** 49.5 kg
> **Range:** 1000-5800 m
> **Maximum flight speed:** 550 m/s
> **Operating altitudes:** 0-4000 m
> **Operating temperature range:** ±50° C.

HERMES-A Air to Surface/Air to Air Missile System – The Hermes-A was designed to bestow upon modern scout/attack helicopters the ability to engage a variety of target sets ranging from current and projected main battle tanks, lightly armoured vehicles, fortifications, engineered structures such as bridges, a large diversity of other surface target types and to provide an air to air capability against low-velocity airborne targets. The system is intended to significantly increase the overall combat capability of the host helicopter through increased engagement range and destructive power of the warhead. The increased engagement range reduces or eliminates the time that the launch helicopter is able to be targeted by battlefield air defence systems by decreasing the engagement parameters within which the host helicopter can be engaged.

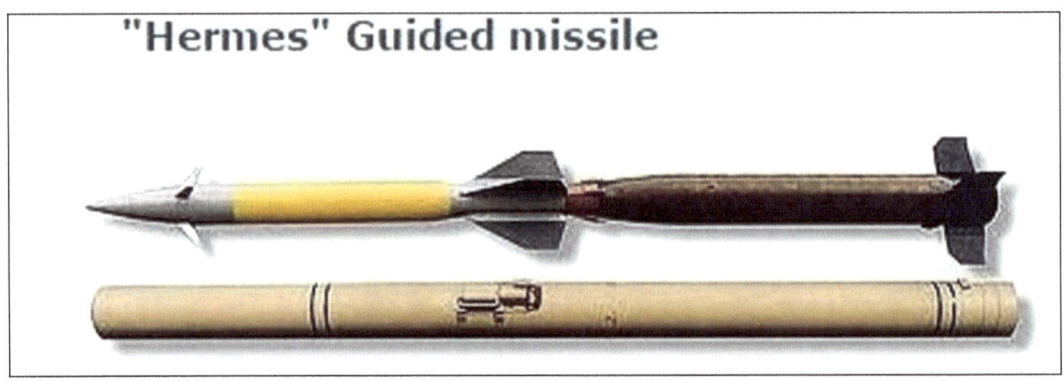

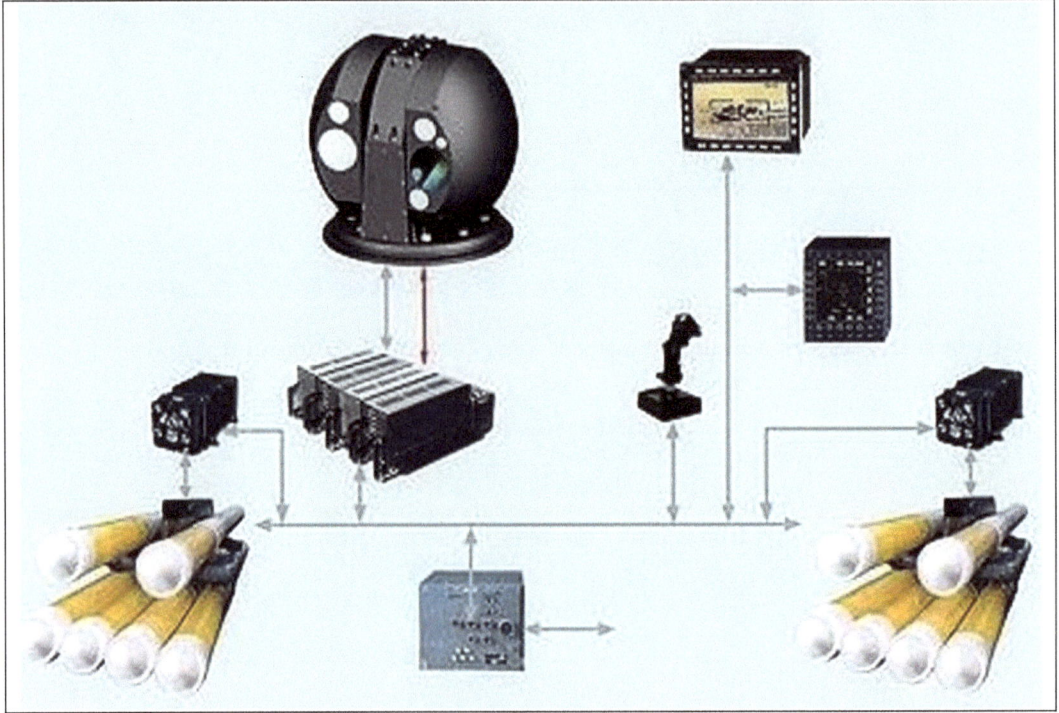

Top: Hermes guided missile. Above: The guidance suite for the Hermes guided missile complex. KBP Tula

The Hermes multi-purpose guided missile is stored in a sealed container through its service life with no requirement for routine maintenance. Once launched the missile is guided by inertial or radio-command in the cruise stage of the flight with a switch to homing in the terminal phase of the flight. Smaller targets can be destroyed by a single missile and large, wider area targets, can be engaged at critical points with either single or multiple missile launches. The system, which features high automation of operation, incorporates a high targeting rate with the ability to salvo fire two missiles against two separate targets; the supersonic speed of the missile, as noted above, reducing vulnerability to counter action through the short flight time and reduced reaction time available for defence systems.

The guidance system features a comprehensive optronic suite that includes TV and IR (Infrared) channels, two channels for laser target designation and an electronics unit incorporating a duel-channel target auto-tracker, a monitor screen and a joystick for day/night automatic tracking and laser illumination of the target.

Hermes-A complex performance specification – data furnished by KBP Tula

Maximum firing range: 15-20 km day/night
Guidance system
    Cruising trajectory stage: inertial or radio-command
    Terminal stage: homing
Guided missile capacity: up to 16

Hermes guided missile – data furnished by KBP Tula

Maximum flight velocity: 1000 m/s
Warhead weight: 30 kg
Warhead type: HEF
Weight of containerised missile: 110 kg
Missile caliber
    Booster stage: 170 mm
    Coasting stage: 130 mm
    Container length: 3500 mm

A Ka-52 launches a salvo of C-80FP 80 mm rockets.

C-80FP 80 mm unguided rocket – The C-80FP 80 mm rocket, which constitutes an element of the armament of a number of tactical fixed wing combat aircraft and armed helicopters, is the primary unguided rocket armament cleared for use by the Ka-52. The C-80FP can be employed against soft-skinned and lightly armoured ground/surface targets and can be launched in single shot or ripple fired, the latter function being of particular use when suppressing enemy fire form a defensive position.

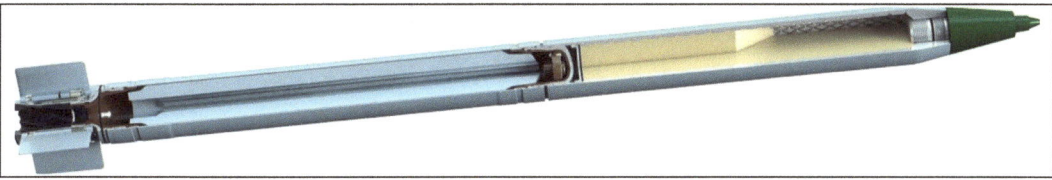

Previous page: Three still sequence of C-80FP 80 mm rockets being launched from a Ka-52. This page top: A Ka-52 launches a salvo of C-80FP unguided rockets. Above: Illustration of the C-80FP 80 mm unguided rocket. MODRF/Rostec/Splav

C-80FP 80 mm rocket – data furnished by JSC Alloy

Caliber: 80 mm
Length: 1400-1500 mm
Range: 6000 m
Warhead type: high explosive penetrating
Warhead weight: 9-9.5 kg
Weight of explosive: 2.5-2.9 kg
Mass predetermined fragment: 3-6 г
Fuse: pin dual-mode
Power plant: high-energy solid fuel rocket motor
Operating temperature range: -54 to +60 C

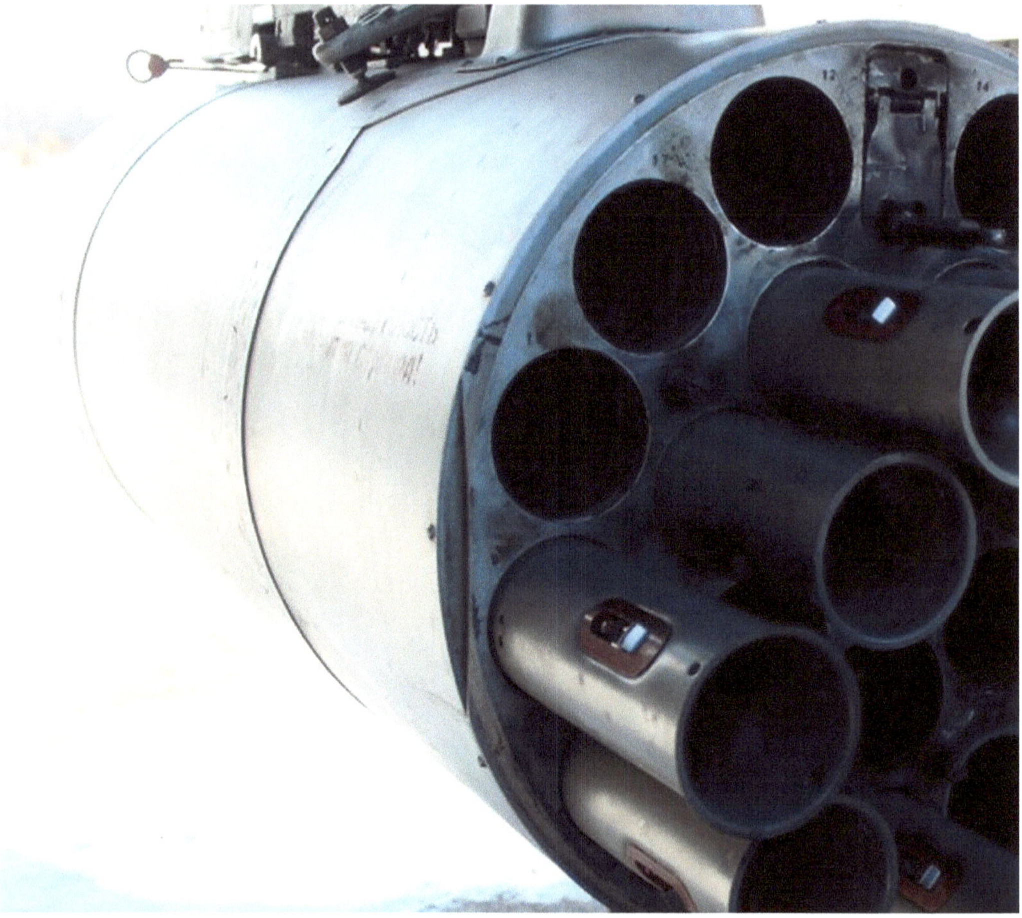

ПРОВЕРЬ НАДЕЖНОСТЬ
ЗАКРЫТИЯ СТОПОРА!

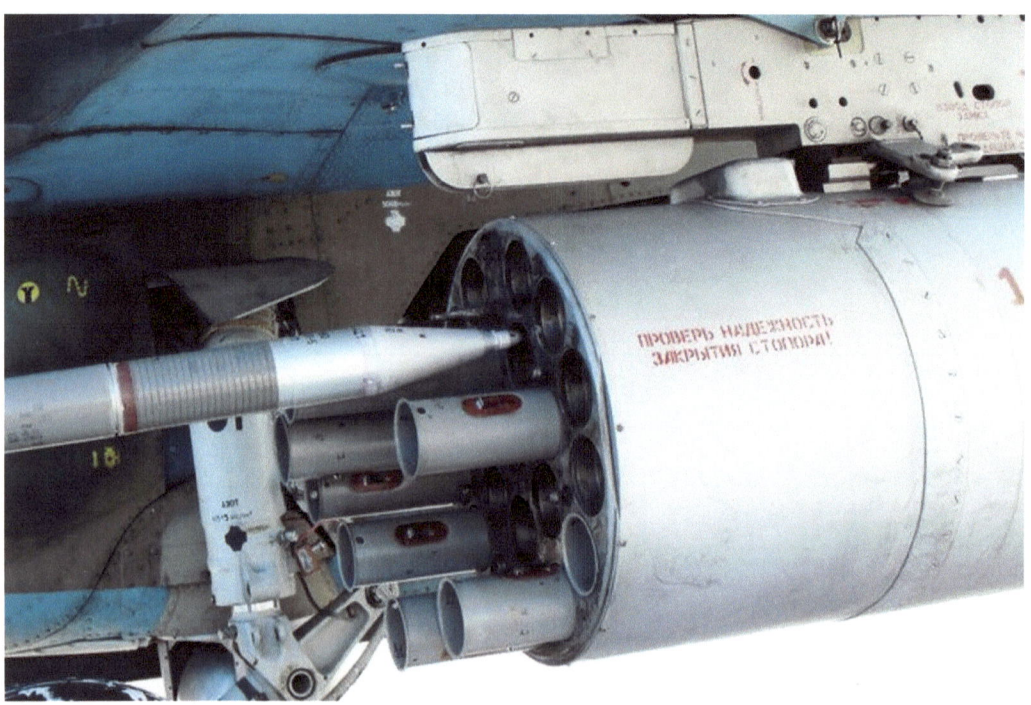

Previous page: S-80FP 80 mm unguided rocket launchers. Top and above: S-80FP 80 mm unguided rockets salvo launched from Ka-52 helicopters. MODRF/Rostec

Block B13L1 rocket complex – This helicopter launched unguided rocket complex, developed by JSC GosMKB Vympel, accommodates five 122 mm rockets that can be employed against soft-skinned and light to moderately armoured targets. The B13L1, which is an armament option on Mi-24 variants and the Mi-28N attack helicopters, can be cleared for employment on the Ka-52. The system can be utilised in single and salvo launch modes, each launcher unit able to conduct up to 70 rocket launches before requiring repair. The complex can be employed in temperatures of ±60° C and in conditions of fog/mist, low atmospheric pressure and solar radiation.

As previously noted it is speculated that the Ka-52K may, with modification, be able to operate with heavy weaponry such as the Kh-35E long range-anti-ship missile. It is further considered that the Arbalet complex could detect average size ships at ranges out to 200 km. While such a weapon option may be attractive to potential export customers, it is seems unlikely to be adopted in the near term for the planned Russian Naval Aviation fleet of Ka-52K's as Russia, as of early 2018, has not indicated an anti-ship role for the Ka-52K – this of course may be subject to change.

Other than weapon options the other major external loads that can be carried are external fuel tanks (currently the inner wing stations are plumbed for external fuel tanks) and stores carriage pods. Another potential role for the Ka-52K is that of a rescue vehicle, whereby the Ka-52 could be employed to drop rescue equipment to personnel in the water.

A Ka-52/C-80FP live fire. Rosoboronexport

4

KA-52/K SERVICE ENTRY & OPERATIONAL DEPLOYMENT

While development of the Ka-52 continued, leading to state trials, production standard Ka-52's were built from 2008. The certificate of acceptance for the Ka-52 to enter service in the Russian armed forces was signed in November 2011. The Russian Federation Air Force had begun to deploy, in small numbers, Ka-52 helicopters to units when, in December 2010, the 334th Tactical Deployment Center, based at Torzhoh, received a batch of three such aircraft from an initial batch of twelve built at the Progress Plant in Arseniev (Russian Helicopters). This was followed by deliveries to Russian operational squadrons, the recipient units being predominantly located in Russia's Eastern, Western and Southern Military Districts, the latter two regions being where the perceived threat to Russia's borders from NATO expansion is foremost. In Russian Federation service the Ka-52 is operated by the Aerospace Forces, the air force component of the Air and Space Forces formed on 1 August 2015 the Air Force and Air Defence Forces were combined to form the Aerospace Force. Although there are still references to the Russian army in regards to Ka-52 helicopters, these assets, have, since 1 August 2015, been combined into and administered by the Aerospace Forces (MODRF).

It is unclear how many Ka-52/K will ultimately be built for Russian Federation domestic service. The 2017 production schedule called for delivery of fourteen Ka-52's that year, joining a not insignificant number of aircraft delivered since the start of the decade. The production contracts in place in 2018 called for a total of 146 Ka-52's to be delivered for domestic use by 2020 (Kret). The first example for an unspecified export customer was built at the Progress Plant in 2017. Under early 2018 planning, serial production of the Ka-52K is scheduled to commence at the Progress Plant in 2020. Initially planned to operate from the Mistral helicopter carriers, the Ka-52K component would have consisted of a deployed group of eight aircraft, alongside a component of eight modernised Ka-29 assault transport helicopters, although planning called for basing sixteen Ka-52K helicopters onboard, presumably at the expense of all or most of the Ka-29 component, if operational requirements called for same (Russian Helicopters). However, it is unclear what the air group of Russia's planned domestic build helicopter carrier fleet would be, assuming the acquisition of such vessels goes ahead. In 2018, it is clear that the Progress Plant has firm orders for 32 Ka-52K to be built for Russian Naval Aviation despite the uncertainty how many, if any, of the planned helicopter carrier fleet will be procured for the Russian Federation Navy (Kret).

Interest in the Ka-52K has been noted from a number of countries from Latin America and the Asia-Pacific regions. It has been stated in Russian Helicopters documentation that the interested parties have provision for development of helicopter carriers, but currently lack a helicopter manufacturing industry, although this is a rather ambiguous statement (Russian Helicopters).

Ka-52 RF-91126 of the Russian Aerospace Forces in the Eastern Military District. MODRF

As the Ka-52 was establishing itself in Russian Federation service the design was becoming more acquainted with national and international trade shows where demonstrations of some of the designs outstanding manoeuvrability was provided. The Ka-52 demonstration flight crew at the 2013 Paris Air Salon was Kamov Design Bureau test crew Alexander Cherednichenko and Mikhail Pavlenko, both praising the side-by-side seating layout for the cockpit as this was considered to have the advantage of reducing workload compared with the single crew Ka-50. One of the pilots would be responsible for flying the aircraft whilst the other was responsible for sensor and weapons management – both crew able to take on either role.

Cherednichenko attributed the direct movement controls to be akin to that of a tactical jet aircraft as opposed to a helicopter while Pavlenko pointed out that the co-axial configuration provided 10-15% additional power over a single rotor configuration. This, as touched upon above, can translate into higher altitude performance, faster climb rates and the ability to carry a heavier payload. Control of the vehicle is further improved by the two-rotor configuration tendency to 'compensate for bank and sideslip' (Russian Helicopters/Pavlenko). Helicopters of the conventional single-rotor configuration tend to 'fly with a bank of 2 or 3 degrees and slight sideslip. This helicopter flies without bank and sideslip. It seems unimportant, but it makes piloting and targeting easier and improves hit accuracy' (Russian Helicopters/Pavlenko).

A Ka-52 of the Aerospace Forces component of the Russian 4th Army in South Ossetia. MODRF

Demonstrations are useful for highlighting such areas of performance as maneuverability. Other areas can be further developed through training exercises and operational deployments. Russian Aerospace Forces combat helicopters, in small numbers, have been operating against ISIL (Islamic State of Iraq and the Levant) and other Syrian opposition forces as elements of the Russian Federations efforts to defeat such in the Syrian Civil War, which, particularly from 2014, took on the mantle of an international conflict. The Ka-52 and Mil-28N operated mainly in central Syria supporting Syrian Arab Army operations to liberate the historical cultural site of Palmyra, which had a strategic significance as a hub to many of the major conflict zones in Syria, including the bastion of Deir-ez-Zor in the East of Syria.

Ka-52 scout/attack helicopters during a training operation with **Mi-8** assault transport helicopters in the Khabarovsk territory of the Russian Eastern Military District. MODRF

Top: A Ka-52 operating in the Russian Southern Military District. Centre and above: Ka-52 helicopters during a rehearsal for a Military Parade flyby in St Petersburg, **Russia** MODRF

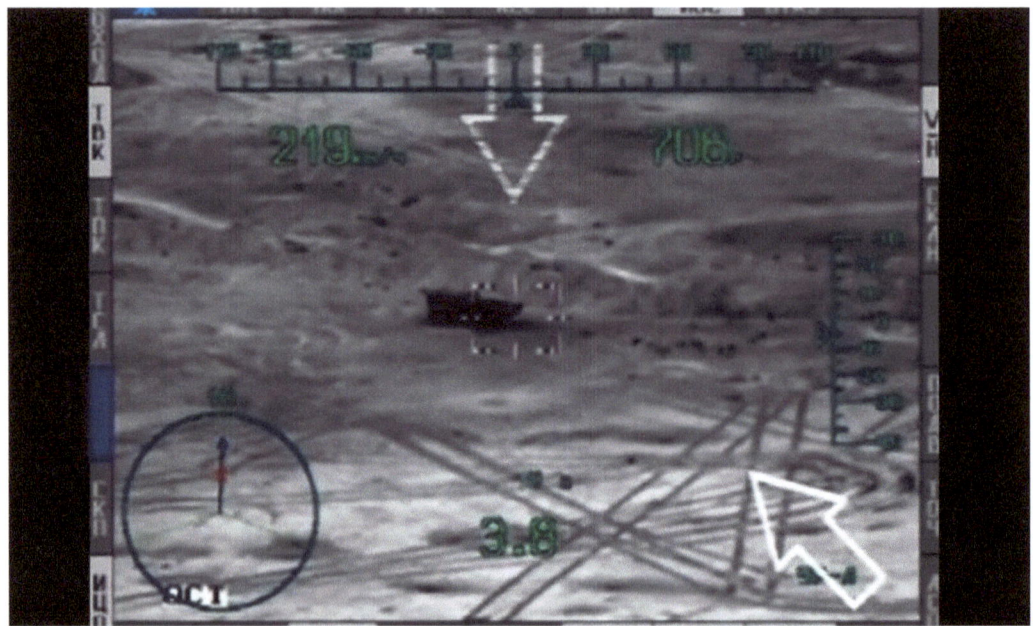

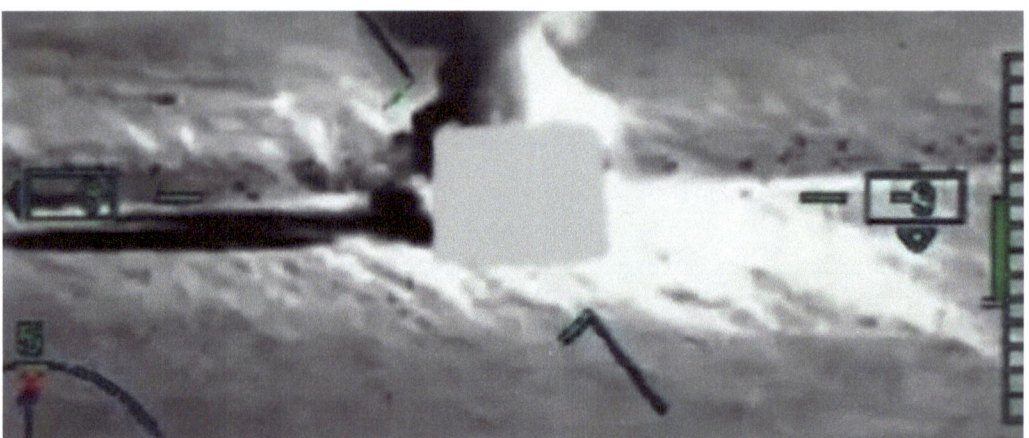

The video still (top) comes from footage of a Mil-28N attack on an ISIL armoured vehicle in the vicinity of Palmyra in 2016. The still above comes from footage of a Ka-52 strike on an ISIL armoured vehicle during the Night heli-borne assault operation to capture the settlement of El Kder as part of the offensive to liberate Deir ez Zor. The blanked out portion in the centre of the still has been necessitated to remove video symbology. MODRF

In late 2016, the Russian Federation dispatched a naval task force to Syria. This force was centered on the Aircraft Carrying Heavy Cruiser *Admiral of the Fleet of the Soviet Union, Kuznetsov*. The air group consisted of a mix of Ka-27PL ASW helicopters, Ka-27PS search and rescue helicopters, Ka-31 AEW (Airborne Early Warning) helicopters (unconfirmed), Su-33 fleet air defence fighters, MiG-29KR (and possibly KUBR) multidimensional strike fighters and a small group of two Ka-52K scout/attack helicopters. Although details of the *Kuznetsov* group strike operations are sparse, the Chief of the General Staff of the Russian Armed Forces, General of the Army, Valery Geriasimov, as noted in chapter 2, confirmed that the aviation assets had been involved in operations leading to the 'liberation of Aleppo', but it is understood that missions were flown against ISIL and or other opposition targets in other parts of Syria. In early 2018, it remains unclear the generality of the main area of operations or indeed the number of sorties flown by the two Ka-52K's – it is known that the *Kuznetsov* air group flew a total of 420 operational sorties, during which more than 1,000 targets were struck, these including command facilities, groupings of enemy forces and fixed fortified fire positions. Due to implementation of a shaky ceasefire the operation of the *Kuznetsov* group was terminated on 6 January 2017.

In early August 2017, ISIL was in steep decline all over Syria as a result of the pressure being applied by the Syrian Army backed by Russian air power. This pressure had the effect of drawing ISIL forces away from North and North eastern areas of Syria allowing the spuriously named US led western coalition backed KDP (Kurdistan Democratic Party – Kurdish rebels and a large contingent of foreign mercenaries funded and supplied militarily by some major western powers and their Middle East allies) to occupy those lands. The Syrian/Russian operations would be the catalyst for launching new offensives that would result in ISIL, as a coordinated fighting force, being driven from much of Syria. As the Syrian Army advanced on Deir-ez-Zor ISIL forces continued to redeploy from northern regions to counter this threat. This would lead to the fall of Raqqa to KDP forces backed by coalition air power, and the occupation of large swaths of land all but abandoned by ISIL.

While the Raqqa sideshow was continuing in the North of the country, Syrian Army units encircled and destroyed large formations of ISIL forces on the road to Deir-ez-Zor. In one such operation, more or less ignored wholesale by the western media, which took place on the night of 11-12 August 2017, Syrian army units were airlifted by helicopter to a point behind ISIL defences 'in the rear of the Iglovites near the settlement of El-Ked' in Raqqa province (MODRF). This was the first large scale helicopter borne assault conducted during the Syrian civil war. The ISIL forces were severely mauled by the Syrian Arab Army forces and Russian air strikes, including support from the handful of Ka-52 helicopters, allowing the main ground force to advance on El Qder. The destruction of ISIL as an organized fighting body in these areas allowed the Syrian army to rapidly advance at 30-40 km per day in the race to Deir-ez-Zor (this was a race with KDP forces filling the void left with the large scale withdrawals of ISIL forces to meet the Syrian army offensive), liberating the large towns of El-Khom, Br-Kdem and capturing the Memnis oil field before encircling ISIL forces in the area of Te-Teiba. Around the same time Syrian army units liberated Sukhne to the east of Palmyra (MODRF).

The above description of operations of the Syrian army in the second week of August 2017 serves to show the role of the Russian Ka-52 and the Mi-28N attack helicopters in the Syrian conflict. Statistics for sorties flown in the above operation and earlier operations have not been forthcoming, but operational video footage clearly shows the Ka-52 detachment successfully engaging and destroying a number of ISIL armoured vehicles, including MBT (Main Battle Tanks).

The Ka-52 role of reconnaissance entails not only data transmission back to a ground station, but also the ability to transmit such data to other helicopters and combat aircraft in the operational area , for example handing targets to one or more Su-25SM ground attack aircraft. There is no information available as to whether or not such a role has been undertaken during the operational deployments in Syria.

During 2016-2017, further deliveries of Ka-52's allowed for the re-equipment of additional units and increased complement of aircraft for existing units. The Southern Military District helicopter regiment, based at Krasnodar Krai, received around 20 Ka-52's in 2016 - crew training was conducted at the Centre of Combat operation and Retraining in the Tver region. In 2017, the Western Military District received some Ka-52 and Mi-28UB helicopters. By early 2017, the increasing supply of modern combat helicopters allowed a like increase in training for one of the Ka-52 primary roles, providing cover and support for Mi-8AMTSh assault transport helicopters, this becoming a major preoccupation for Ka-52 helicopter operations in the Western and Eastern military districts, experience feeding into the operations in Syria. The Southern Military District Ka-52 crews conducted training flights in mountainous regions during 2017.

The introduction of significant numbers of modern Ka-52, Mi-28N/UB attack helicopters, modern variants of the Mi-24 (Mi-35M) attack/assault transport and Mi-8AMTSh armed assault transport helicopters have produced a quantum leap in capability of the Russian Federation tactical helicopter fleets. This has allowed advanced helicopters to support expeditionary warfare groups like that deployed to the Syrian Arab Republic from 2015 and those providing a formidable capability to counter the Russian perception of a growing threat to her borders from NATO expansion in the western and southern regions.

Previous page and this page top: Ka-52 helicopters of the Eastern Military District. Above: A Ka-52K flies in proximity of the Aircraft Carrying Heavy Cruiser, *Admiral of the Fleet of the Soviet Union, Kuznetsov* **circa 2016/2017.** MODRF

**Top: Ka-52 helicopters of in the Pskov region of Russia's Western Military District.
Above: Ka-52 helicopter of the Russian Eastern Military District.** MODRF

GLOSSARY

AEW	Airborne Early Warning
AIM	Airborne Interception Missile
ARK	Air Rescue Kit
ASRAAM	Advanced Short Range Air to Air Missile
ASW	Anti-Submarine Warfare
ATGM	Anti-Tank Guided Missile
Az	Azimuth
C	Centigrade
DIA	Defense Intelligence Agency
DRFM	Digital Radio Frequency Memory
GPMG	General Purpose Machine Gun
H	Height
HE	High Explosive
HEAT	High Explosive Anti-Tank
HMTDS	Helmet Mounted Targeting Designation System
hp.	Horsepower
HUD	Heads up Display
I	Roman numeral number 1
IFV	Infantry Fighting Vehicle
II	Roman numeral number 2
III	Roman numeral number 3
IIR	Imaging Infrared
Il	Ilyushin
INS	Inertial Navigation System
IR	Infrared
IRIS-T	Infrared Imaging Seeker –Tail Control
ISIL	Islamic State of Iraq and the Levant
JSC	Joint Stock Company
K	катран (Katran)
Ka	Kamov
KDP	Kurdistan Democratic Party
kg	Kilogram
kgf	Kilogram force
Km	Kilometer
km/h	Kilometers/per hour
kN	Kilo newton
LMG	Light Machine Gun
m	Metre
MANPADS	Man Portable Air Defence Systems
MBT	Main Battle Tank
Mi	Mil

MiG	Mikoyan
Millirad	A unit of measurement of radiation dosage
mm	Millimetre
MODRF	Ministry of Defence of the Russian Federation
NATO	North Atlantic Treaty Organisation
NVG	Night Vision Goggles
ODS	Onboard Defence System
OJSC	Open Joint Stock Company
RF	Radio Frequency
SLR	Self-Loading Rifle
Su	Sukhoi
TNT	High Explosive formation
TsAGI	Central Aerodynamic Institute
TV	Television
USAF	United States Air Force
USSR	Union of Soviet Socialist Republics
V	Volt
V[e]	Velocity
W	Watt
WCSH	Weapons Control Systems for Helicopters
-	Minus
+	Plus
x	Times multiplication
±	Plus or minus
~	Approximately equal to (can also be used to mean asymptotically equal)
°	Degrees

ABOUT THE AUTHOR

Hugh Harkins, FRAS is a historian and author with an extensive background in astro/geophysics and studies/research in the wider scientific, aeronautic, astronautic and nautical technical and historical fields. Hugh has published in excess of sixty books; non-fiction and fiction, writing under his given name as well as utilising several pseudonyms. He has also written for several international magazines, whilst his work has been used as reference for many other projects ranging from the aviation industry, international news corporations and film media to encyclopaedias, museum exhibits and the computer gaming industry. Hugh is a member of the Institute of Physics and is an elected Fellow of the Royal Astronomical Society. He currently resides in his native Scotland. Other titles by the author include:

Iskander - Mobile Tactical Aero-Ballistic/Cruise Missile Complex
Orbital/Fractional Orbit Bombardment System - The Soviet Globalnaya Raketa
Counter-Space Defence Co-Orbital Satellite Fighter
Sukhoi T-50/PAK FA - Russia's 5th Generation 'Stealth' Fighter
Sukhoi Su-35S 'Flanker' E - Russia's 4++ Generation Super-Manoeuvrability Fighter
Sukhoi Su-34 'Fullback'
Sukhoi Su-30MKK/MK2/M2 - Russo Kitashiy Striker from Amur
MiG-35/D 'Fulcrum' F – Towards the Fifth Generation
Air War over Syria, Tu-160, Tu-95MS & Tu-22M3 - Cruise Missile and Bombing Strikes on Syria, November 2015-February 2016
Sukhoi Su-27SM(3)/SKM
Russian/Soviet Aircraft Carrier & Carrier Aviation Design & Evolution Volume 1 - Seaplane Carriers, Project 71/72, Graf Zeppelin, Project 1123 ASW Cruiser & Project 1143-1143.4
Heavy Aircraft Carrying Cruiser
Light Battle Cruisers and the Second Battle of Heligoland Bight
British Battlecruisers of World War 1 - Operational Log, July 1914-June 1915
Eurofighter Typhoon - Storm over Europe
Tornado F.2/F.3 Air Defence Variant
Air to Air Missile Directory
North American F-108 Rapier - Mach 3 Interceptor
Convair YB-60 - Fort Worth Overcast
Boeing X-36 Tailless Agility Flight Research Aircraft
X-32 - The Boeing Joint Strike Fighter
X-35 - Progenitor to the F-35 Lightning II
X-45 Uninhabited Combat Air Vehicle
Into The Cauldron - The Lancaster MK.I Daylight Raid on Augsburg
Hurricane IIB Combat Log - 151 Wing RAF, North Russia 1941
RAF Meteor Jet Fighters in World War II, an Operational Log
Typhoon IA/B Combat Log - Operation Jubilee, August 1942
Defiant MK.I Combat Log - Fighter Command, May-September 1940
Blenheim MK.IF Combat Log - Fighter Command Day Fighter Sweeps/Night Interceptions, September 1939 - June 1940
Tomahawk I/II Combat Log - European Theatre, 1941-42
Fortress MK.I Combat Log - Bomber Command High Altitude Bombing Operations, July-September 1941
XF-92 - Convairs Arrow